MISSIONS BY THE BOOK

MISSIONS
BY THE
BOOK

*How to Find and Evangelize Lost People of
Every Culture on Every Continent*

Tom Stebbins

Christian Publications
Camp Hill, Pennsylvania

Christian Publications
3825 Hartzdale Drive, Camp Hill, PA 17011

Faithful, biblical publishing since 1883

ISBN: 0-87509-656-5
LOC Catalog Card Number: 95-83058
©1996 by Christian Publications, Inc.
All rights reserved
Printed in the United States of America

96 97 98 99 00   5 4 3 2 1

Unless otherwise indicated,
Scripture taken from the
HOLY BIBLE:
NEW INTERNATIONAL VERSION®,
©1973, 1978, 1984 by the
International Bible Society.
Used by permission of
Zondervan Publishing House.
All rights reserved.

Dedication

This book is dedicated as a memorial to my late sister, Ruth Thompson, and her late husband, Ed, who while serving the Lord as missionaries in Banmethuot, Vietnam laid down their lives during the Tet Offensive, February 1, 1968. On the first anniversary of their untimely martyrdom, I placed on Ruth's bunker grave the following Scripture which aptly describes their death and subsequent fruitfulness:

Except a corn of wheat fall into the ground and die, it abideth alone; but if it die, it bringeth forth much fruit.
(John 12:24)

Contents

Foreword

I t is my pleasure to point out the unusual combination of features of this very valuable book.

Most important, in one sense, is the fact that it reads like a fast-paced novel. It will get read. But is it worth it?

It is studded with marvelous personal anecdotes—what a memory Tom has!—that always faithfully throw light on a systematic series of unfolding perspectives on Vietnam. Through his prose, he details the work of one of America's most outstanding mission agencies in that difficult field and, in turn, illuminates the fundamental drama of God's work in our world today. This in itself is obviously even more important than its readability.

Enhancing its value is the fact that from beginning to end it is a true story packed with rewarding insights into the very nature of a missionary family. In the process it becomes almost a practical handbook on how to raise children!

I actually believe it will be a wonderful book

for use in family devotions. I would like to see families with smaller children (who need an exciting book to keep their attention) set aside some time once a week when, together, they can fellowship in His presence. Reading one chapter a week like that would be a fine way to develop a sense of togetherness as they witness the unfolding drama of God's work in the lives of the Stebbinses. With its 13-chapter structure, of course, it could equally well be used in Sunday schools.

Here, in a single book, is a fine, wholesome, instructive story about the cause of missions and the very real human factors that global cause involves. I would hope every home could have a copy and enjoy its worth. In addition it will have many other uses, I am sure. What a valuable textbook it can be in the Christian college setting. This is a good book!

Ralph D. Winter
General Director
U.S. Center for World Mission

Author's Preface

Vietnam has received plenty of bad press over the past four decades. It is the land of my birth (to American missionary parents) and the land where I myself served for 20 years as a missionary. You won't be surprised if my slant on Vietnam is different from that of the American GIs who fought the war and the news people who covered it.

I was born in the imperial capital of Hue—in a French hospital on the banks of the beautiful Perfume River. As a boy I shook hands with Emperor Bao Dai. I saw the land and its charming people at the peak of Vietnam's glory.

My missionary service coincided with the war years. I witnessed the awful pangs of America's ugliest war. The day South Vietnam finally fell to the invading northern armies, I was there. A few hours later, standing on the deck of the S.S. Vancouver, I looked through my tears to the shoreline of the land I so dearly loved. Through clenched teeth I cried out, "O God, why? Why did You allow this to happen?"

It has taken me another 20 years to try to come up with some kind of an answer. That's part of my reason for writing this book. Another part, as the title suggests, is to offer a biblical rationale for missions. I have tried to slant the book to the seminarian and the college student of missiology. I have kept in mind as well the lay Christian who wants to know what the Bible has to say about this important subject.

Since my earliest years, God's Word was "the Book" of my life. Every evening, my missionary father gathered his family around the supper table for family worship. I must admit that the Bible at first did not impress me very positively. I considered it a dead, dry book of genealogies, antiquated stories, dull poetry and unrealistic demands.

At age nine I trusted Christ as my Savior. But no one helped me discover assurance through the Bible. In my desperation, I "went forward" at church services and summer camp meetings, time after time, hoping the emotional experience would somehow supply what I lacked. Then at age 16, while attending a summer youth conference at Nyack (New York) College, I enthroned Christ as Lord of my life. I began reading through the New Testament, chapter by chapter.

A few weeks later, my missionary parents returned to Vietnam, and I took up life at a boarding school in Florida. There I continued my daily Bible reading. And the Bible began to come alive.

This is amazing! I thought to myself. *Where have I been all these years? This Book is exciting!* I fell in love with the Bible. I couldn't put it down. When dorm lights went out at bedtime, I dived under the blanket to read by flashlight. In the pages of the Bible I discovered a new purpose and standard for living. I found a source of nourishment, growth and clean living. I took Psalm 119:9 as my theme verse: "How can a young man keep his way pure? / By living according to your word."

In my college years another verse—Psalm 16:11—found its way into my heart, promising direction, joy and eternal hope: "You have made known to me the path of life; / you will fill me with joy in your presence, / with eternal pleasures at your right hand."

As my wife, Donna, and I prepared to leave for missionary service in Vietnam, God's Spirit impressed upon us another passage from the Psalms which became our life verse. It promised us a fruitful, fulfilling missionary career: "He who goes out weeping, / carrying seed to sow, / will return with songs of joy, / carrying sheaves with him" (Psalm 126:6).

That was the spring we met Dawson Trotman, founder of The Navigators. We met him at a missionary conference in Boston's Park Street Church. During the week that Daws and we were together, I made a commitment that I have pursued ever since: to listen, to read, to study, to meditate on, to memorize and to obey God's Word. Has not God said, "All Scripture is God-breathed and is useful for teaching, rebuking, correcting and training in righteousness, so that the man of God may be thoroughly equipped for every good work" (2 Timothy 3:16-17)?

You will not have read too far in this book before you discover it is not just another missiology text. True, you will discover in it basic missionary principles. But essentially it is the story of my personal commitment to and ministry according to the Book of books. It is a testament of how at every juncture in my life and ministry that Book gave me strength, direction, hope and the secrets of fruitfulness and fulfillment. Over and over, in a world of confusing voices, I found myself saying with Simon Peter, "Lord, to whom shall we go? You have the words of eternal life" (John 6:68).

One more purpose motivated me to write this book. The psalmist expressed it this way: "Since my youth, O God, you have taught me, / and to this day I declare your marvelous deeds. / Even when I am old and gray, / do not forsake me, O God, / till I declare your power to the next generation" (Psalm 71:17-18).

My purposes, then, are four: (1) To tell *my* side of the Vietnam story; (2) To share what God through His Word has taught me about missions; (3) To show through personal anecdotes from my missionary life how God's marvelous deeds reflect the truths of His Word; (4) to declare to following generations God's mighty power.

My sincere thanks goes to H. Robert Cowles, who has served as editor for this book as well as my two previous books. Bob has the gift of sensing what I am trying to say and couching my thoughts in appropriate English. He and I are long-time friends. Without his help I would not have dared a project like this.

I invite you now to turn to Chapter One. In that opening chapter I try to explain why a young couple would leave comfortable, safe America to spend what turned out to be 20 difficult, dangerous years as missionaries to Vietnam—a land that would be rent by horrible bloodshed and war.

You may be surprised by what you read!

Thomas H. Stebbins
Ft. Lauderdale, Florida
November, 1995

Chapter One

A Passion for the Lost

Luke 15

O N APRIL 30, 1975, I ESCAPED VIETNAM from the roof of the U.S. Embassy aboard a helicopter. Hours later, the country of my birth and boyhood, the land where I served as a missionary fell to the communists.

Three weeks earlier my wife, Donna, and I had flown by Pan Am jet to the safety of the Philippines. But then I learned that more than 500 of my Vietnamese friends and coworkers faced almost certain death or imprisonment. I felt compelled to return to Vietnam to seek an escape route for them.

By then, all commercial flights into Vietnam had ceased, and no civilian was allowed aboard the military aircraft going in. It took a cable from the White House to the commanding general at Clark Air Force Base in the Philippines to get me on my way.

Enemy troops already surrounded the Saigon airport. To avoid antiaircraft fire, our lumbering C-130 cargo plane was forced to descend to the runway in a tight corkscrew. Two hours later, communist artillery and mortars destroyed the airport, effectively closing that major door into and out of the country.

Once off the plane, I made my way as quickly as possible to the U.S. Embassy. My mission: to beg the vice-ambassador to help my 500-plus Vietnamese friends escape.

The vice-ambassador was sympathetic. But by then the airfield was in ruins. That meant the U.S. government was limited to the use of small helicopters able to land on rooftops or parking lots. The odds of adding 500 more people to the long list of those already scheduled for evacuation were not encouraging.

I knew I would find my friends gathered at the International Protestant Church not far from the embassy. I hurried over there to meet with them. I told them the prospects were not good, but I promised to do everything possible to find a way out for them. Already sporadic machine gun and small arms fire was spraying the streets. As I returned to the embassy, I saw that marines had barricaded the embassy street with barbwire. Gingerly I made my way through the barricade and dashed to the embassy. The gates were locked! An unarmed Vietnamese guard who had not left his post of duty helped me climb over the wall to safety.

For the next 30 hours frantic mobs surrounded the embassy. United States marines held them off at gunpoint, allowing only those with proper documents to enter. Since I knew Vietnamese, I volunteered as an interpreter. I also helped organize the 2,000 evacuees inside the embassy who had gathered to board the 50 helicopters shuttling between the embassy and a ship in the harbor.

Finally, at 1:00 a.m., April 30, as enemy invaders pressed ever closer to the heart of Saigon, the embassy doctor came out to me in the courtyard.

"Tom," he said, "you've gotta board the next chopper. The ambassador will be on the one that follows. *Tell your friends at the church that there's a ship at the docks that will take them to safety. But they'll have to hurry!*"

There was still hope for my 500 Vietnamese friends! Not by helicopter but by ship! Quickly I telephoned to the church to tell the gathered group this good news—this way of escape. *"But you'll have to hurry!"* I added with urgency. Then I took an elevator up six floors to the embassy roof and joined the group still waiting for evacuation.

As the heavily loaded helicopter skimmed the tree tops just beneath us, I wondered if a communist machine gun would blast us out of the sky. Moments later, however, we were safely down on the deck of the *S.S. Vancouver.*

Next stop: Manila and, for me, my anxious wife.*

Why Missions?

Often since then I've been asked, "Tom, whatever motivated you to risk your life like that?"

I can only reply, "They were my friends. *Their* lives were at stake. I was concerned."

That answer is appropriate to another question: "Why missions?" People continue to ask, "Why should I involve myself in world missions?"

The fact is, people's lives are at stake. Not their physical, earthly lives (though missionaries frequently can render temporal help as well). Why missions? Because people's spiritual, eternal lives are at stake. That is the thesis of this opening chapter. People are lost! And without the Savior, Jesus Christ, they will be lost forever, throughout all of eternity.

Luke 15 is one of the great missionary chapters of the Bible. It's a record of three stories Jesus told: the story of a lost sheep, the story of a lost coin and the story of a lost son. Each object was valuable to the person involved. Each needed to be found.

Luke informs us that Jesus told the stories in response to comments by the Pharisees and the

---

*   For more on this story, see the appendix

teachers of the law. These Jewish leaders "muttered, 'This man welcomes sinners and eats with them.' " But Jesus had more than Pharisees and teachers of the law in mind. A little later Jesus would say of Himself, "The Son of Man came to seek and to save what was lost" (Luke 19:10). And still later He declared to His followers: "As the Father has sent me, I am sending you" (John 20:21). We hardly can escape the conclusion that *God wants His church to seek and to save a lost world.*

I am a former missionary. I continue to be very active in evangelism, both in America and internationally. I see four threads running through these narratives Jesus told: *a lost people, a loving search, a lavish celebration* and *a lethargic church. Let's trace these four threads through the chapter and see their clear application to the missionary task.*

1. A Lost People

Note that Jesus was surrounded by a large crowd of people. "Now the tax collectors and 'sinners' were all gathering around to hear him" (Luke 15:1). In His day, they were not exactly socially desirable. We would consider them the irreligious. They were the spiritually confused, the morally bankrupt.

And off to one side was the small huddle of Pharisees and teachers of the law—observers. They were commenting among themselves that this Teacher, who called Himself God's Son, was befriending sinners.

Jesus, able to read their very thoughts, launched out on these three back-to-back stories. It was as though He was saying to the Jewish religious leaders (and to us today), "I'm going to clear up this matter once and for all. I never want there to be any more confusion on this issue. Lost people are important to Me and to My Father."

Throughout history the secular world has taken a jaundiced view of the human species. Homer complained, "Among all creatures that breathe on earth . . . there is not anywhere a thing more dismal than man." A "degraded mass of animated dust," wrote Byron. "A poor creature halfway between an ape and a god," commented William Ralph Inge. Author Jean Girandeaux thought that people were but "timid punctuation marks sprinkled among the incomprehensible sentences of life." "Nature's sole mistake," commented W.S. Gilbert.

Atrocious descriptions, are they not? But God continues to regard humankind as the crowning wonder of His creation! We really matter to God. In fact, we matter so much that He became one of us in order to redeem us. And He is pleased to live in the hearts of us whom He has redeemed.

How much do people—lost people—mean to you? Suppose next Sunday morning someone were to poll all the worshipers in your church. Whom do they consider important to God? Whom do they consider unimportant? Would the "Important" column bear the names of a few political figures, maybe some of the movers and shakers in business and a handful of Christian celebrities? I hope it would include your pastor and some of the faithful workers without whom any church could not survive.

What about the "Unimportant" column? Would most of the people you know fall into that column? Would the "Unimportant" list be considerably longer than the "Important" list?

If the truth were known, I suspect that most of us have an unconscious list of people whom we feel aren't very important to God. Drug peddlers, child pornographers, abortion doctors, greedy stockbrokers, crooked attorneys. It likely includes most of those who voted against our candidate in the last election! And all that mass of faceless humanity in Africa, the Middle East, Asia and South America who seem perpetually trapped in revolution, natural disasters and drug operations. Surely God isn't very concerned about them, so why should we be?

Certainly Jesus' three stories about the lost sheep, the lost coin and the lost son must have caught the attention of those religious observers. Gathered in their "holy huddle," they had condemned Jesus for hanging out with undesirable sinners. I wonder if they were moved by the concept of a loving God who could look beyond sin to treasure the sinner. He is a God who says, "Even though you've gone astray and got yourself lost, you are important to Me!"

World missions was born in the heart of a God who loves people. The shepherd had affection for his lost sheep. The woman prized her lost coin—possibly part of her wedding dowry. The father loved his lost son. So God loves people who are lost—lost in trespasses and sin.

Let people come to really understand that a person apart from Christ the Savior is eternally lost. Let them truly understand this and their hearts will melt. World missions will come alive.

World missions never gripped my heart until I came to understand the meaning of Jesus' amazing claim. He said, "I am the way and the truth and the life. No one comes to the Father except through me" (John 14:6). Did you see it? "No one." Jesus is the only Way. Millard Erickson states it very succinctly:

1. All humans are sinners, by nature and by choice, and are therefore guilty and under divine condemnation.

2. Salvation is only through Christ and His atoning work.

3. Belief is necessary to obtain the salvation achieved by Christ. Therefore, Christians and the church have a responsibility to tell unbelievers the good news about Jesus Christ.

4. Adherents of other religions, no matter how sincere their belief or how intense their re-

ligious activity, are spiritually lost apart from Christ.

5. Physical death brings to an end the opportunity to exercise saving faith and accept Jesus Christ. The decisions made in this life are irrevocably fixed at death.

6. At the great final judgment, all humans will be separated on the basis of their relationship to Christ during this life. Those who have believed in Him will spend eternity in heaven, everlasting joy and reward in God's presence. Those who have not accepted Him will experience hell, a place of unending suffering, where they will be eternally separated from God.[1]

The Red Bobo tribesman in West Africa who prostrates himself toward Mecca and pleads to Allah for mercy is lost! The Hindu in India who religiously, faithfully, hugs to his breast his wooden god is lost. The devout grandmother in Peru, fingering her rosary, if she doesn't know Christ as her Savior, is lost. The ancestor-worshiper in Vietnam who reverently places fruit and flowers on the family altar is lost!

Peter was convinced there was no alternate way of salvation. Of Jesus he said, "Salvation is found in no one else" (Acts 4:12). He added, "There is no other name under heaven given to men by which we must be saved" Paul concurred. He said, "No one can lay any foundation other than the one already laid, which is Jesus Christ" (1 Corinthians 3:11). People separated from God by sin who've never trusted Christ—or, worse, have never heard of Him—are lost!

This lostness was indelibly impressed upon me during my first term as a missionary to Vietnam. One day I followed a pagan funeral procession to the cemetery. At the house neighbors of the family helped lower the body into a crude casket. They added sand to serve as a seal against odor, then nailed the lid on tightly. Some 20 men lifted the casket onto bamboo poles which they hoisted to their shoulders. As the procession left for the cemetery, flutists and drummers led the way down the village path. The family, dressed in white with rags tied to their hair, followed behind the coffin, hands gripping the end of the casket. The entire procession marched to a deafening drumbeat and the screech of flutes. Women wailed. Children cried.

At the cemetery the casket was lowered gradually into the ground. The drums beat louder and the pitch of the flutes rose. Mourners pounded their breasts and wept more pitifully than before.

I cannot forget that hopeless scene. It was as though the demons of hell were stomping on the casket, crying, "Down, down, down to hell, piteous soul!" As I went to bed that night, I kept hearing in my mind the drum beat and the cries. Worse, I kept imagining the torment of the one who had died in his lostness. Had he and his family had opportunity to hear of Jesus Christ? Had any Christian made an effort to share with him the good news of Jesus?

That brings me to the second thread in Jesus' narratives:

2. A Loving Search

In Jesus' stories it is evident that the lost sheep, coin and son mattered very much to the shepherd, the woman and the father. The shepherd went in search of his sheep. The woman stopped all else to look for her coin. The father, wisely knowing that his wayward son must himself resolve to return home, nevertheless gazed longingly in hopes he would come.

Jesus was saying to the Pharisees and teachers of the law that those with whom He was associating mattered to God. They mattered so much that He—Jesus—was making every effort to "find" them. Jesus wants us to see, too, how much He cared. He wants every one of us to join hands with Him in an all-out search for lost people wherever they are!

One reason I chose to serve with The Christian and Missionary Alliance is its long-standing purpose to search for the lost—especially among the unreached people groups of the world. In my earlier Evangelism by the Book, I described one such search. That unforgettable privilege bears repetition here.

Taking off from Saigon airport, our pilot nosed the single-engine Fairchild Porter northwest across South Vietnam's delta. He gained altitude as quickly as possible to avoid sniper fire from below, for Vietnam was at war.

Tom, I said to myself, this could be your last day on planet earth! But my apprehension about flying over enemy-held territory was checked as I remembered again my mission. I was en route to take the good news of Jesus Christ to tribal villages that had never heard of Him.

Gradually the multi-checkered rice paddies below us blended into dark green rows of rubber trees. These, in turn, became majestic, jungle-covered foothills marred only by the craters and landslides left from American B-52 bombing raids.

My preoccupation with the panorama below us was abruptly halted as the pilot cut the engine and began his descent to the little provincial capital of An-Loc. Shortly we were bumping across the landing strip. Pastor Dieu-Huynh, driving a borrowed Jeep, was there to meet me.

Dieu-Huynh was one of a handful of Stieng Montagnards who had believed in Christ Jesus while studying to become government cadres. Concerned about the destiny of his 100,000 fellow tribespeople, Dieu-Huynh deliberately gave up his plans for civil service and instead enrolled at Nhatrang Biblical Theological Institute to become a pastor-evangelist.

Upon his graduation in 1970, he visited me at our Saigon mission headquarters. He invited me to help him evangelize the first Stieng villages.

"But Dieu-Huynh," I countered, "I don't speak your tribal language. What help can I be?"

The young preacher waved off my hesitancy. "That's no problem," he assured me. "You preach in Vietnamese, and I'll interpret into Stieng."

It was an invitation I could not refuse. And now I was fulfilling it. I climbed into the Jeep with Dieu-Huynh, who coaxed the aging vehicle over the nondescript provincial roads toward the four Stieng villages we were scheduled to visit. As the vehicle groaned over the crest of a particularly steep hill, I spied in the distance the first village. Smoke was rising from each of the longhouses built on stilts to protect from mosquitoes and tigers.

The sound of our approaching Jeep attracted a crowd of bare-breasted women and naked children, soon joined by G-stringed men. Some snickered at their first sight of a white man. Others looked on in wide-eyed wonder. By the time we had set up our battery-operated public address system, some 200 villagers had gathered under the shade trees in the center of the village.

Dieu-Huynh greeted the people in their own language. I could not understand what he was saying, but clearly he had the attention of the villagers. I assumed he was introducing me, for he ended his comments by handing the microphone to me.

At last, my dream of pioneering an evangelistic thrust into one of the world's remaining unreached tribes had come true. I could hardly believe it! The message I had prepared seemed suddenly inadequate. How should I begin? What could I say to people who had never even once heard the beautiful name of Jesus Christ, my Savior?

I kept the message simple enough for a five-year-old to grasp. Sentence by sentence, Dieu-Huynh interpreted for me. The people seemed to understand. I could tell by the look on their faces. But had I said enough? What kind of a response should I expect? Should I invite them to trust in my Savior?

Unsure what to do, I said falteringly, "If you'd like to receive God's Son as your Savior, please stand." To my surprise, all my listeners, to a person, rose to their feet!

"Dieu-Huynh," I said, "I'm afraid they don't understand. Have them sit down again while we clarify for them what is involved in such a commitment."

Then, for the second time, I extended the invitation. Again, everyone stood. Puzzled, I asked Dieu-Huynh to explain the gospel further and to pray with them in small groups.

In the next village, I preached the same message. No one responded. The people were not yet ready to give up their ancient animistic ways. Likewise, in the third village, people were not yet ready to follow Christ.

The sun at high noon was very warm when we reached the fourth site. So the villagers invited us into their makeshift palaver house. They sat shoulder-to-shoulder on the mud floor, knees tight under their chins, the backs of one row up against the knees of the next.

The bearded, balding village chief sat in the very center of the crowd. In the intense heat, I could see the perspiration pouring from his body. But neither the heat nor the press of people seemed to matter. Everyone was intent on what I had to say. It was the first time they had heard such good news. Their excitement was undeniable.

As I extended an invitation to these Montagnards to put their faith in Jesus Christ, the unexpected happened. The chief, who served as spokesman for the village, stood up. He shook his fists in the air, at the same time shouting something at the top of his lungs. The villagers responded in like fashion.

"What are they shouting?" I asked Dieu-Huynh.

He explained. "You asked, 'Who wants to trust Jesus Christ as Savior?' And they are shouting, 'We do! We do!' "

Never before or since have I witnessed such an enthusiastic response to the gospel. And to think this was happening in the mountain jun-

gles of Vietnam in a village that had never before heard of Jesus! Despite the heat, chills
coursed from the top of my head to the very
ends of my toes. It had to be the most thrilling
day of my life!

Sometime in eternity, I believe I will look
back through the corridors of time to that day
and say to God, "Thank You for such a privilege!"

Seeking the Lost Is Costly

It costs to seek the lost. My sister Harriette
and her husband, George Irwin, spent 28 years
in the highlands of Vietnam searching for spiritually lost tribespeople. It meant mastering
three difficult languages: French, Vietnamese
and Koho. It meant driving over incredibly
rough, dangerous roads in tiger-infested jungle
mountains. It called for long, uncomfortable
hours sitting cross-legged on mats in smoke-
filled longhouses. It included extended separa-
tions from loved ones back home, from
children at boarding school and sometimes
from each other.

Donna and I, working in the lowlands of Vietnam among the Vietnamese population, also
found the search costly. Our first 18 months we
had only bicycles for our travel. Imagine bicy-
cling at midday in Florida in August! And the
villages to which we went were often distant.
Sometimes we were forced to wade through
chest-deep rivers. Sometimes we slept beneath

a coconut tree on army cots under mosquito nets.

Then there was the illness. At least twice I was near death with malaria. All of my first term I had painful boils. One day Donna accidentally pricked her thumb as she was changing the baby's diaper. The next day her thumb was swollen from infection. By the third day the French doctor, to prevent life-threatening gangrene, had to remove the tip of her thumb bone.

Later there was the constant danger of Vietcong rockets, of mined roads, of sniper fire and guerrilla attack.

There is cost in seeking the lost wherever they are. On a short-term missions trip to Gabon, Central Africa, our team traveled all day on roads so bad we suffered seven blow outs. I was given a tour of the mission hospital at Bongolo. The hospital serves the deep interior of Gabon. No words can describe the sights and smells.

I can't take an hour of this! I thought to myself. But the doctors and nurses serving that hospital endure the sights and smells day after day, year after year.

I took a missions team to Manila for an Evangelism Explosion leadership training clinic. The air pollution—most of it from horrendous traffic jams—was unbelievable! I was told about one veteran missionary who retired after serving long in Manila. Her doctor remarked that her lungs looked as though she had been a lifetime chain-smoker!

Yes, there is cost to searching for lost people. Is it worth the cost? I think you know the answer. It will be evident as we follow the third thread running through Jesus' three stories in Luke 15.

3. A Lavish Celebration

When an object of great value is lost—a sheep, a coin or a son—there is great sorrow. But when at last that object is found, there is great rejoicing! The greater the value, the more lavish the celebration.

The shepherd finds his wandering sheep and throws a party. The woman finds her lost coin and gathers her friends and neighbors for a time of rejoicing. The father welcomes home his wayward son and calls for "the best robe" and a ring for his boy's finger, sandals for his feet and the "fattened calf." The happy father made sure there was a proper celebration to mark his son's repentance and return!

Did you know there was a celebration when you trusted Christ as your Savior? Rejoicing erupted in heaven! Jesus said, "I tell you, there is rejoicing in the presence of the angels of God over one sinner who repents" (Luke 15:10). All heaven broke into praise as your name was written in the Lamb's book of life. That's because you matter so much to God.

That same lavish celebration filled heaven's courts when Mrs. Ung Tham trusted Christ in

Ho-Chi-Minh City (Saigon). She and her husband, the great-grandson of one of Vietnam's emperors, studied English at our youth center in Hue, the imperial capital. Every Friday evening for three years she heard the gospel proclaimed in both English and Vietnamese. She sang English choruses and read English tracts and Gospels. Donna and I visited in her home, sharing personally with her God's message of salvation. But because of her strict Buddhist upbringing and her family ties to royalty, she resisted.

When Vietnam fell in 1975, her family fled to Ho-Chi-Minh City. Far from the Buddhist stronghold of Hue, she felt more free to search for the truth. She wrote me, requesting the words and music of the choruses she used to sing at the Hue Youth Center. She asked for the address of a local church she could visit.

You can imagine my joy and Donna's when later she wrote to say she had trusted Christ and had been baptized! Since then, some of her children have come to Christ. And her husband is showing a greater interest in spiritual matters. The joy over just one such "sinner who repents" is sufficient reward for all our 25 years of missionary service. It would have been worth everything we went through for just that one lost person, Mrs. Ung Tham, to be found!

Why missions? Because it's one of the most rewarding and fulfilling vocations on earth! As lost Dani tribespeople in Irian Jaya, Indonesia, lost Bobo tribespeople in Mali, West Africa, lost

Auca tribespeople in Ecuador, lost Hmong in Laos, lost Cantonese in Hong Kong, lost Hispanics in Miami repent and turn to Christ, those who have reached them with the good news join the angels of heaven in lavish celebration!

Thus far we have followed three threads in Jesus' stories in Luke 15: a lost people, a loving search and a lavish celebration. There is one more important thread we must not overlook. It appears in both the context of these stories and in the conclusion to the story of the prodigal. The best word I can find to describe this thread is lethargy. Luke 15 is a warning to you and me lest we become part of . . .

4. A Lethargic Church

That Israel's spiritual leaders were lethargic is evident from their disapproving comment about Jesus: "This man welcomes sinners and eats with them" (Luke 15:2). We find that same unconcern in the petulant actions and words of the prodigal's older brother. Note how Jesus described the older brother's response to the lavish celebration that followed the prodigal's return:

> Meanwhile, the older son was in the field. When he came near the house, he heard music and dancing. So he called one of the servants and asked him what was going on. "Your brother has come,"

he replied, "and your father has killed the fattened calf because he has him back safe and sound."

The older brother became angry and refused to go in. So his father went out and pleaded with him. But he answered his father, Look! All these years I've been slaving for you and never disobeyed your orders. Yet you never gave me even a young goat so I could celebrate with my friends. But when this son of yours who has squandered your property with prostitutes comes home, you kill the fattened calf for him!"

"My son," the father said, "you are always with me, and everything I have is yours. But we had to celebrate and be glad, because this brother of yours was dead and is alive again; he was lost and is found." (15:25-32)

Jesus does not say what response the older brother made to his father's plea. Could He have left the story open-ended in hopes of a favorable response from the Pharisees and teachers of the law? Was He hoping for a favorable response from you? The older brother had two options: he could join the party, or He could be a party pooper. And those are the options open to us.

Shortly after I became associate pastor for outreach at Christ Community Church in

Omaha, a woman attending our new members class expressed amazement at our church's commitment to world missions. She then went on to tell me a little about the church from which she was transferring her membership. She said that all of that church's offering income went to its general and building funds. The church had a missions goal of $500 that particular year, but nothing had been contributed to it! It was an apathetic, lethargic church.

Dr. Carl L. McMindes, president of the Gospel Missionary Union, states, "In 1990, North American evangelicals gave about 2.5 percent of their income to the work of the Lord. Some estimate that about 0.4 percent went to world missions."[2]

"Overall, we are losing the battle to evangelize at a rate of 23,561 every day," asserts World Pulse.[3] There are more people now who have never heard the gospel than at any time in history.

Millions of those yet to be reached are identified with distinct blocs of people: Muslims, Hindus, Buddhists, animists. The difficulty of access may not be geographic so much as political, social, religious, cultural and linguistic. Add to these the accessible but unreached. If Jesus is the Way and the only Way, all these unreached are lost unless they put their faith in Jesus Christ. But "how can they believe in the one of whom they have not heard? And how can they hear without someone preaching to them?" (Romans 10:14).

What is your attitude toward these who are lost, whether in other lands or at home? As a believer, is your heart broken by their lostness? Do you pray for them with tears? Do you give until it hurts that they may hear the gospel? Are you prepared, if God should call, to go to them with the message of hope?

What are you doing to accelerate missionary advance into countries or areas where lost people wait to be found? Are you involving your family? your church? Is the church where you worship zealous for the lost? Or are the members lethargic and lukewarm?

Missions—missions by the Book—involves searching for, finding and saving lost people of every culture and on every continent. Dying people must find Christ, the Life! People groping in pagan darkness must see Him who alone is the Light. Lost people, whatever the cost, must be found.

I left the U.S. Embassy in Saigon on the third-from-last chopper out of that stricken city. My last act before leaving had been to contact my 500 Vietnamese friends waiting at the International Protestant Church. I relayed the good news that a ship still at the docks could take them all to safety—if they hurried.

A few weeks later, on Guam, I met the Vo-thanh Thoi family, who had been at the church. They told me that as soon as they heard of the rescue ship, they jumped into their Volks-wagon. They sped across town to the port and boarded the ship to safety.

"But what about the hundreds who were waiting with you?" I asked.

"Oh, they didn't believe they could reach the ship. They decided to wait for a helicopter."

My heart ached. "They didn't believe." I had risked my life to provide them an escape route. For want of faith, they had failed to take advantage of it.

In the ensuing communist takeover some of them died, some were imprisoned; all suffered under the heavy hand of the new regime.

Before you move on to the next chapter, let me ask you to do something that may open a whole new chapter in your life. Get down on your knees with your Bible open to Luke 15. Then ask God to speak to you by His Spirit. Let Him speak not just about the Why? of missions but about the How? of your personal involvement.

For He does want you to be involved!

Study Guide Questions

1. What would motivate a Christian to commit his or her life to world missions?

2. What biblical evidence do we have that lost people matter to God? How much would you say they mean to Him?

3. How much do lost people matter to you? What have you done, are you doing or do you plan to do to reach lost people around you for Christ? to reach those in other lands or cultures?

4. What is your local church doing to reach lost people in other cultures and lands? What more do you see that you or your church could be doing?

5. What biblical evidence is there that people outside of Christ will be eternally lost? Cite three specific Bible verses.

6. What did it cost God to seek and save lost people? What is it costing you? What is it costing your local church congregation?

7. In the parable of the lost son, what was the response of the older brother to the celebration party? How did the story apply to the Pharisees and teachers of the law? How might it apply to members of your local church?

8. According to Carl L. McMindes, what percentage of evangelicals' 1990 charitable giving went to world missions? How does your giving to missions compare? How does your local church's missions giving compare?

9. Have you ever thought about serving overseas or cross-culturally? What is keeping you from committing yourself to career missions? to a short-term missions project?

Endnotes

1. Millard, J. Erickson, The Evangelical Mind and Heart (Grand Rapids: Baker Book House, 1992): 130-131.
2. "AD 2000: More Than a Slogan?" The Gospel Message, 1992, No. 2): 15.
3. World Pulse, (13 December, 1991), vol 26 no 23.

Chapter Two

Selected, Set Apart, Sent

Jeremiah 1:1-10

"WELL, TOMMY, WHEN YOU GROW UP will you be a missionary like your father and grandfather?" How many times, as a child, did my parents' well-meaning friends meet me with that question! Doctors' children often choose the medical profession and carpenters' sons frequently become carpenters. People expect that missionaries' children will become missionaries. And a surprising number do.

But *I* had no intention of conforming to statistics. I had a ready answer for those who questioned me, and I delivered it without apology.

"Me? A missionary? Not I! That's the last thing on earth I'd want to be!"

It wasn't that I was rebellious. But I had been through some rough times in Vietnam. As a child I almost died of malaria. And I had suffered from scores of boils. I had sat in unbearable heat and humidity through interminable, boring Vietnamese church services. Doing more of that as a vocation did not appeal to me.

Rather, I dreamed of being a farmer. I wanted to drive a tractor and milk cows. Later, in my early teens, I became enthralled with tennis. I set my sights on becoming a tennis pro or a coach. Practicing every possible moment with the team at Nyack (New York) High, I rose rapidly to rank second in Rockland County.

In 1949, after eight years in the States, my parents headed back to Vietnam. They offered me a choice. I could return with them to attend Dalat School, then in Vietnam, or I could remain in the States and finish secondary school at Hampden DuBose Academy. Hampden DuBose was a Christian boarding school in Zellwood, Florida. Children of missionaries and of many Christian leaders across America attended Hampden DuBose.

As I glanced through the school's yearbook, I saw photos of horses, waterskiing and—best of all—tennis courts! In my mind Florida was tennis heaven! My choice was obvious.

Little did I realize at that moment that Hampden DuBose would not be preparing me for a future in tennis. Rather, it would become the place where God set my course in the direction of world missions.

To do so God used His Word—a passage in Jeremiah and another in Ezekiel—to lead me into His will. I want you to look with me at

Jeremiah 1:1-10. Notice the four steps in God's plan for Jeremiah—steps I found applicable in my life. Maybe they will fit *your* situation as well: 1. God *selects,* 2. God *sets apart,* 3. God *sends.* And 4. God *speaks* through those He sends. Let's begin with the first.

1. God Selects

The word of the LORD came to me,
saying,
"Before I formed you in the womb I
knew you . . ." (1:4-5)

The statement is amazing. Before Jeremiah was even conceived, God selected him to be a prophet. The word *knew* in Hebrew also means *chose.* God foreknew Jeremiah from eternity past and chose him. God even selected his form and his family.

The word *formed* is the same Hebrew verb used when we're told God "formed the man from the dust of the ground" (Genesis 2:7). Think of that for a minute. God was as directly involved in the formation of Jeremiah as He was in the creation of Adam! Some would suggest that we are the result of a chance meeting of a sperm and an ovum in our mother's womb. Don't be too sure of that. *God* designed us. He intended that we have these bodies just as He formed them. I thank God often for His formation—bald head, bridges and bifocals included! I praise Him that I am "fearfully and wonderfully made" (Psalm 139:14). Can you say the same? Do you recognize God's process of formation in your life and praise Him for it?

God also selected Jeremiah's family. We're told he was the "son of Hilkiah, one of the priests at Anathoth" (Jeremiah 1:1). What a godly heritage he must have had! Certainly it was a great preparation for his future ministry.

I thank God for selecting the family in which He placed me and for the godly heritage He gave me. My grandfather, John Hartman, was a contemporary of Albert B. Simpson, founder of The Christian and Missionary Alliance. For a time my grandfather served as an honorary vice-president of the organization. Grandpa Hartman entered missionary service through a rather unusual course of events. A Methodist layman from Barbados was miraculously healed during one of Dr. Simpson's services at the New York Gospel Tabernacle. Impressed by the breadth and depth of the Alliance message and ministry, this Methodist layman appealed for Alliance missionaries to be sent to the Caribbean.

John Hartman, with his wife and daughter, went. The Hartmans launched what proved to be a very fruitful ministry. My mother, Mary Hartman, was born two years later—one of six children in all. Grandpa Hartman spent 17 years in the Caribbean. Some 10,000 people professed faith in Christ. Four thousand of them were baptized and folded into 35 churches, known as the Christian Mission. Most of those churches are still in existence today. You can find them throughout the Caribbean.

In 1908, concerned for the education and welfare of his children, my grandfather left the Caribbean to take a pastorate in Providence, Rhode Island. For some years he taught at Boston Bible Institute with V. Raymond Edman and Merrill C. Tenney. Dr. Edman later became president of Wheaton College, and Dr. Tenney later directed the Graduate School at Wheaton College.

Many years ago I heard Dr. Edman relate an interesting incident concerning my Grandfather Hartman. My grandfather was scheduled to travel to the island of Martinique to visit a small, struggling group of believers. With a woman's intuition, my grandmother pleaded with and prevailed upon him not to go. As it turned out, a volcano erupted, wiping out the island's population save for one survivor in an underground dungeon.

When my grandfather heard this tragic news, he wept over the fate of the small band of believers. Later he learned that a few days before the volcano, the little band of Christians had left Martinique. Faced with the islanders' continued resistance to the gospel and gross immorality, the Christians had followed Jesus' injunction to "shake the dust off your feet when you leave" (Matthew 10:14).

But *they*, knowing my grandfather's schedule, supposed *he* had perished on the island. It was a happy reunion when he and they met, each providentially spared from the judgment on Martinique.

Heirlooms are important to most people. The only treasures passed down to me from my Grandfather Hartman were a few faded photos and a two-inch stack of personal letters written to my mother, Mary Hartman Stebbins, when she was a missionary serving in Vietnam. From those letters I have learned some valuable lessons. One of the most significant was from a passing reference my grandfather made to his prayers. He prayed daily that God would save all of his children and grandchildren. He prayed that they would find appropriate places of service in the Lord's vineyard.

Over a span of 13 years my mother gave birth to seven children. I was the youngest, born in the imperial capital of Hue, Vietnam. Our home life made two deep, lasting impressions on me. One was my mother's love—love for her husband and children and love for the Vietnamese people expressed in many practical and sacrificial ways. The other was my father's devotion to the Word, prayer and evangelism. There is no way to overestimate the impact these godly role models made upon my character and ministry.

But as committed as Dad was to missions, he never tried to directly influence me to pursue a missionary career. Many times I heard him say, "I don't want any of you children to become missionaries—unless God calls you. Of course, if God calls you, I would be delighted!" And delighted he was when God led six of us into missionary service.

But, how exactly did God lead me into full-time missionary service? Answering that question takes us back to Jeremiah 1 and step two of God's leading.

2. God Sets Apart

Before you were born I set you apart;
I appointed you as a prophet to the
nations. (1:5)

In 1941 the Japanese invaded Vietnam—then called French IndoChina. Without firing a shot, they took over the country from the French. Our family of nine fled to the Philippines. A month later, aboard the *S.S. President Pierce*, we proceeded to the United States. Ours was the last ship to sail from Manila before the Philippines also fell to the Japanese.

For the next few years we lived in Nyack, New York. Mother kept our household operating; Dad was regularly away in missionary deputational work.

Nyack College, where both Dad and Mother had studied, was just up the hill from where we lived. Our very first summer in Nyack, there was a week-long youth conference at the school. Mervin Rosell was the evangelist and Paul Milburn was the song leader. I was too young to be a part of the conference, so Mom sat with me in the balcony.

Each night Merv Rosell asked a very penetrating question: "If you were to die tonight, do you know for sure that you would go to heaven?" Each night, after the question, Mom leaned over and asked me if I knew that for sure. And each night, with a straight face, I lied to her and said I did.

After the final evening of the conference I walked back down to our house trembling. I prepared for bed, but I couldn't sleep. I lay there in the darkness thinking, *What would happen to me if I died tonight? What would happen to me if Jesus returned tonight?* Finally, some time past midnight, I knocked hesitantly on Mom's bedroom door.

"Will you help me receive Christ as my Savior?" I asked. Of course Mom was only too happy to do so. As we knelt together in prayer beside her bed, I asked Jesus into my life. What wonderful peace and joy flooded my young heart! After that, I knew my life would never be the same.

Unfortunately, I didn't grow much during the next years. No one discipled me. No one helped me get into God's Word. Time after time, lacking assurance, I went forward after church services, trying to find at an altar of prayer what I should have been shown in the Word. I'm ashamed to say it, but for seven long years I was a "Sunday Christian," singing in the church choir and playing trombone in the orchestra. The other six days of the week I had no time for God. At school I deliberately hid the fact that I was a Christian.

But God is merciful! That sad state of affairs came to a screeching halt at another summer youth conference held again at Nyack College. Dr. Harold Boon, one of the professors at the school (later he became college president), substituted for the scheduled speaker. His message was tailor-made for me. It was about Peter following Christ from afar, warming his hands at the enemy's fire, denying Christ before a young girl.

Dr. Boon wasn't describing Peter. He was describing Tom Stebbins! *I* was the guilty one. And with Peter I wept bitterly. I repented of the sin and compromise in my life. I asked Christ to become my Lord, to set me apart for holy living, to make me red-hot for God!

A few weeks later, Dad and Mom saw me off on a Florida-bound Greyhound bus for Hampden DuBose Academy. And soon they were en route once more to Vietnam and another term of missionary service.

Hampden DuBose was a very positive experience for me. I want to describe some of my experiences there. But before I do, I feel impelled to ask you two personal but very important questions. Have you let God set you apart? Have you enthroned Jesus as Lord of your life? Before you can really realize God's purpose for you, you must allow Him to take over the controls of your life. You must cut clean of everything that would compromise your standing with God. You must be sold out to Him. If you sense that you've fallen short of a full surrender to God, why not pause right here and yield your life to His lordship over you? Do not miss the blessing God has in store for you.

3. God Sends

> I appointed you as a prophet to the
> nations. . . .
>   You must go to everyone I send you to.
> . . . See, today I appoint you over nations
> and kingdoms. (1:5-10)

Our God is a sending God. He sent His prophet Jeremiah to proclaim His message to the nations. He sent His Son to earth to redeem humankind. Christ sent His Spirit on the day of Pentecost. He sent His apostles to the ends of the earth. And the Great Commission has never changed! For 2,000 years Christ has sent His servants with His gospel to every nation. In every generation He has sought people willing to be sent.

As I mentioned, I was not at first a willing candidate. I had absolutely no desire to follow in my father's or grandfather's missionary foot-steps. In fact, I totally abhorred any thought of spending my life in Christian service, especially in a foreign culture.

But then, in the fall of 1950, youth evangelist Jack Wyrtzen brought his daughter to enroll her at Hampden DuBose. And the school asked this popular founder of the Word of Life Hour to speak to all of us. Jack chose as his text God's words declared through the prophet Ezekiel: "I looked for a man among them who would build up the wall and stand before me in the gap on behalf of the land so I would not have to destroy it, but I found none" (22:30).

Jack aptly applied the text to world missions. Over and over he stated that God was looking for young men and not finding them.

"Where," Jack asked, "are the men? They're all saying, 'Lord, send my sister!' " I had three sisters already serving as missionaries and the fourth preparing to follow. I had been saying in my heart, *Lord, send my sisters but let me stay at home praying for and supporting them!*

Jack went on to comment that there were many more women missionaries than men. Men were badly needed. Then he did some-thing incredibly relevant to me. He pointed in my direction.

"Some of you young men right here in this academy are saying, 'Lord, send my sister.' But God is looking for *you*, and He needs *you* on some mission field of the world!"

At that moment I saw not the finger of Jack Wyrtzen pointing at me, but the finger of God's Spirit. God was taking His Word, taking the Great Commission and applying it personally to my heart.

That day at Hampden Dubose Academy, as Jack Wyrtzen spoke, God called me. As far as I was concerned, it was a crystal-clear call—as explicit as God's call to Jeremiah or to the apostle Paul.

You ask, "What is a call?" It is simply God's applying by His Spirit the Great Commission to an individual's heart and mind. I have interviewed scores of missionaries. I have listened to their testimonies. Although the circumstances and details of their calls are varied, all of them point to one central action. The Holy Spirit applies Christ's mandate to their own hearts.

At the conclusion of his message, Jack Wyrtzen extended an invitation. He asked those of us who felt God's call to serve Him abroad to come forward for a prayer of commitment. Amazingly, about half of my class responded. And it did not stop there. I think everyone of us who went forward has ended up on a mission field somewhere!

Beginning that day, God gave me a consuming passion to take the gospel to lost people. That passion has never lifted! The farming ambition of my childhood and the tennis dreams of my youth were eclipsed for-

ever by God's "You must go to everyone I
send you to."

4. God Speaks

"Ah, Sovereign Lᴏʀᴅ," I said, "I do not
know how to speak; I am only a child."
But the Lᴏʀᴅ said to me, "Do not say, 'I
am only a child.' You must go to everyone
I send you to and say whatever I command you." . . .
Then the Lᴏʀᴅ reached out his hand
and touched my mouth and said to me,
"Now I have put my words in your
mouth." (1:6-9)

Not only is our God a sending God, He is
also a communicating God! He spoke and the
worlds came into being (Hebrews 11:3). In the
past He spoke through the prophets (Hebrews
1:1). Jeremiah was one of them. Then in these
last days He has spoken to us by His Son (Hebrews 1:2), who is called the Word (John 1:14).
And this Word, Jesus Christ, wants to speak
through us, His redeemed people.

But notice that God must speak *to* us before
He speaks *through* us. The word of the Lord
came to Jeremiah in the 13th year of the reign
of King Josiah (Jeremiah 1:2). Jeremiah testifies,
"The word of the Lᴏʀᴅ came to me" (1:4). Jeremiah could not speak God's word until he had
heard God's word.

Early in life I learned the importance of hearing God's Word. Every evening my father gathered his family of nine around the supper table for family worship. At the time the Bible was to me an uninteresting collection of dry genealogies, antiquated stories, dull poetry and unrealistic demands. But after I enthroned Christ as Lord of my life, I began reading through the New Testament, chapter by chapter.

"Amazing!" I exclaimed to myself. "Where have I been? This Book is exciting!" I fell in love with the Bible and couldn't put it down. When dorm lights went out at bedtime, I dived under my blankets to finish my reading by flashlight! In the pages of my Bible I discovered a new purpose in life and a new standard for living. I found a source of nourishment for spiritual growth and the means of holy behavior.

Do you likewise find God's Word important? Did you spend time in it this morning? What has God said to you recently through His Word? If you have a family, are you involving them in Bible reading and prayer?

It was one thing for God to speak to me through His Word. That was exciting! But for God to speak *through* me? That was frightening! Petrifying! I hated public speaking. Every time I had to speak before people I broke out in a cold sweat. My knees buckled. My mouth went totally dry. God was sending *me* to speak? Impossible!

To make matters worse, several months earlier I had suffered a major defeat in public speaking. Like all the other students at Hampden DuBose, I was required to participate in a school-wide declamation contest. I had memorized a speech, "The Last Will and Testament of a Refugee." When it came my turn, I gave the opening line with great gusto. Then my mind went blank. I could recall nothing of what I had memorized. Finally the closing line popped into my thoughts. I blurted it out and sat down, utterly defeated, thoroughly humiliated, embarrassed beyond words. After that ugly debacle, I knew I could never, never become a public speaker!

And now God was calling me to be a missionary, and that certainly included public speaking. What was I going to do? A battle raged! On one hand, there was nothing in all the world I wanted more to do than proclaim the gospel. On the other hand, there was nothing I hated more to do than speak in public.

Then one day, in my chapter-by-chapter reading of the Old Testament, I came to Jeremiah. To my wonder I discovered that this important prophet at first had misgivings about his ability to speak in public. He even got into an argument with God about it. As far as I was concerned, the book of Jeremiah was written just for me! Weren't Jeremiah's words my words exactly? "Lord, I do not know how to speak. I am only a child."

I read on and discovered God's comforting, reassuring promise to Jeremiah: "Do not be afraid of them, for I am with you and will rescue you." And again: "The LORD reached out his hand and touched my mouth and said to me, 'Now, I have put my words in your mouth' " (Jeremiah 1:8-9).

How incredible! God through His Word was telling me that He would help me speak. He would be my Prompter. More important than that, He would speak through me. Could I believe Him to do all of that for me and through me? How could I know for sure?

Then this thought came clearly to my mind. *If God can help me speak someday overseas, why can't He help me right here in school? In fact, shouldn't that be the real test—to prove His promise right here and now?*

Another school-wide declamation contest was approaching. The more I thought and prayed about it, the more excited I became. I asked God to pull me through the declamation contest. And not just somehow. I asked Him to help me reach the contest finals. That was a next-to-impossible request! I told the Lord I didn't care about winning. I knew if I won I'd be too proud to be of much use to God. But being a finalist would be a seal to His promise for my missionary future.

I chose a rather humorous declamation, "Let's Not Pretend." There was nothing particularly biblical or even religious about it. But for me the speech was an intensely spiritual matter between God and me.

I prayed daily and earnestly. I also determined to do everything I could to master the speech. Up and down the football field I paced, reciting the script aloud, over and over. And then I practiced it with gestures before a mirror.

At last, the declamation week arrived, and finally it was my turn to stand before the student body. Many of my classmates remembered my disastrous first attempt and were cheering for me. As I took my place to speak, something unusual happened. It was as though Someone else took over, speaking through me. Every word came clearly to my mind. Not once did I so much as stutter. Impeccably, enthusiastically I delivered the speech right to the end. From the applause as I returned to my seat, I knew I had done fairly well—perhaps well enough to be a finalist.

You can imagine my utter delight and praise to God when, at the end of the week, I was named as one of the five or six finalists! No, I didn't win. But for me it was a victory that confirmed God's call on my life. He had promised to use me in speaking His Word wherever He would send me.

In the years since my student days at Hampden DuBose, I have stood before all types of difficult audiences on every continent except Antarctica. I've spoken in the extremely difficult tonal language of Vietnam. Not infrequently I knew there were communist infiltrators in the audience. Often in more recent years and in other lands I have spoken through interpreters. I've taught nonstop for six to eight hours at a stretch in evangelism seminars and clinics. Just as with Jeremiah, "The LORD reached out his hand and touched my mouth" (1:9).

God will do the same for you. Put Him to the test. Do your part by preparing carefully. The God of Jeremiah is the same today!

The fear of public speaking hounds many people. I'm convinced there are young people who feel God's call to missionary service. But the fear of public speaking causes them to seek out some type of support ministry instead. I do not depreciate support staff. We need secretaries, business managers, school teachers, dorm parents, guest home operators, pilots, doctors, builders and all the others. But if God's call is to proclaim the gospel, trust Him to make you adequate for the task. Remember Jeremiah and the promises God made to that equally reticent young man.

From eternity past, God had a purpose for Jeremiah. God *selected* Jeremiah for a purpose. He *set him apart* for a purpose. He *sent* him for a purpose and He *spoke through him* with a purpose.

The God who fashioned Jeremiah fashioned you. And since He does nothing without purpose, it follows that He brought you into this world for a purpose. Your business is to discover God's purpose. The specifics will vary, but one thing is crystal clear. Wherever you are, whoever you are, whatever you do, be sure God has selected you. He wants to set you apart. He intends to send you. He desires to speak through you.

Like Jeremiah, will you commit yourself to God's purpose?

In eternity we will look back from God's perspective at our years on earth. We'll see how very special we were in His economy. We'll see the work He really wanted us to accomplish. We'll see the lost friends, relatives, work associates and neighbors God longed for us to reach with the gospel of Jesus. We'll hear the words He wanted us to speak. We'll see the people groups of the world He intended us to reach with the good news. We'll see the life plan God wanted us to live out in the years He gave us on earth.

Father God, may we not wait until eternity to discover—then, with deep regret—the plan You intended for our lives. Help us to understand just how special we are to You and to appreciate the plan for which You selected us. Set us apart. Send us. Speak through us for Your glory and purpose. Amen.

Study Guide Questions

1. According to Jeremiah 1, what might be the most appropriate steps leading to a missionary career?

2. What evidence is there in that chapter that Jeremiah was important to God and His

purpose? Is it accurate to assume that each of us is important to God and His purpose?

3. Does the high number of missionaries' children who follow their parents into a missionary career surprise you? What precautions do you feel they might need to consider? What advantages do they bring to a missionary career?

4. In what ways may parents influence their children toward missionary service?

5. Why is the "Lordship of Christ" an important factor in a person's consideration of missions as a career?

6. How would you define a missionary call? How might it differ from, say, the call a person would receive to be a homeland pastor?

7. If God does not call a person to be a career missionary, in what ways can that person support those who are called?

8. Based on Jeremiah 1, God at least sometimes recruits people with no apparent ability to fulfill the assigned task. Why? Can we always expect God to step in and make up for our lack?

9. Do you agree that God has a purpose for everyone, yourself included? What do you understand to be God's purpose for you? What are you doing to fulfill that purpose?

Chapter Three

An Eternally Significant Definition

Second Corinthians 5

CHARLES HADDON SPURGEON, THE FAMOUS London preacher, once warned, "Beware of labels. Too often they're fables." Certainly you are familiar with the old adage, "You can't tell a book by its cover." And I would add that you can't always believe the sign out front of the business.

One day in congested Hong Kong I was looking for a supermarket where I could shop. As I drove around I finally saw one with a large *Park and Shop* sign out front. *This is great!* I thought to myself. *I can park the car off the street and take my time shopping!* But there was one problem. I couldn't find any parking lot! Finally I stopped the car in front of the store, left the motor running and

47

dashed in to ask the owner where his parking lot was.

"Parking lot?" he asked. "We don't have any! Just park anywhere along the street."

"But your sign says I can *park* and shop!" I protested.

"Never mind the sign," the storekeeper responded pleasantly. "It doesn't mean what it says."

That storekeeper's nonchalance toward the inaccuracy of his sign is matched and exceeded by another. In our society and worldwide, people carelessly misuse and misunderstand the word *Christian.* It has become perhaps the biggest fable, the greatest misnomer of our day. *It doesn't mean what it says.*

For that reason, before we go any farther, we need to take time for an eternally significant definition. We need to define the term *Christian.* A proper understanding of this term may determine your eternal destiny. Certainly it will greatly affect the impact of your missionary outreach. The reason is simple. *Christian* is the "bottom line." Making Christians is the point of our missionary work.

Actually, the word *Christian* (little Christ or Christlikeness) does not surface until several years into the church era. We are informed, "The disciples were called Christians first at Antioch" (Acts 11:26). The term could have been spoken first in derision. Or, as some counter, it may have been coined by Greek believers, for whom the term *disciple* fell short of fitting all that followers of Christ were supposed to be. King Agrippa used it. He said to Paul, "Do you think that in such a short time you can persuade me to be a Christian?" (Acts 26:28). Peter, writing to fellow Jewish believers going through difficult times, said, "If you suffer as a Christian, do not be ashamed, but praise God that you bear that name" (1 Peter 4:16). In the first century *Christian* was a sacred and meaningful term, an eternally significant name!

Unfortunately, today the term has lost most of its original flavor. It has come to mean different things to different people. Ask a man if he is a Christian, and he may respond, "Of course! I go to church. I'm law abiding. I'm good to my neighbors." Or he may take offense and retort, "What do you *think* I am—a *heathen?*"

In the Near East I discovered that a person who is a non-Jew or a non-Arab is automatically classified a Christian. They use the word almost ethnically, racially. To others *Christian* is simply an adherent of a specific religion, just as others are Buddhists or Hindus.

God's Word alone is qualified to define the word Christian *for us.* I can think of no better place to turn than Second Corinthians 5. There the inspired Paul gives us one of the most precise yet practical definitions of *Christian* that can be found anywhere.

In the first half of this letter to the Corinthians Paul uses several rich, graphic metaphors to describe Christians. He calls them "the aroma of Christ" (2:15), "a letter from Christ" (3:3), those "being transformed into [Christ's] likeness" (3:18), people with "an eternal house in heaven" (5:1), "a new creation" (5:17), "the temple of the living God" (6:16). He calls himself and those with him "Christ's ambassadors" (5:20) and "servants of God" (6:4). Three of the metaphors are in Chapter 5—one of my all-time favorite Bible chapters. It is there that I invite your attention. Using Second Corinthians 5, I want to consider the Bible's definition of *Christian* under four headings: the *meaning,* the *miracle,* the *marks* and the *ministry* of a truly biblical Christian.

1. The Meaning of a True Christian

As far as the Bible is concerned, a Christian is one who is related to Jesus Christ. "If anyone is in Christ, he is a new creation" (5:17). Paul does not say, "If anyone is a citizen of a predominantly Christian nation . . ." or "If any man is a member of a Protestant or a Catholic church . . ." or "If anyone keeps the 10 Commandments and follows the Golden Rule. . . ." He says we must be "in Christ."

That means we must be vitally related to Christ. It means that we are in Christ and Christ is in us. But, you ask, how can I be both in Christ and at the same time have Christ in me? You can't have it both ways. It is one or the other!

To that I reply, "How can a glass be in the ocean and at the same time the ocean be in the glass? It's the same way with Christ. The Spirit of Christ pervades our beings. Christ is our center, our circumference and the very substance of life itself to us. He is our Savior and our Sovereign. He is everything!

"As a branch is in the vine, drawing its very life from the stem, so we are in Christ, drawing our very life and love from Him, serving Him, looking forward to the day when we will be with Him in person forever!"

Are you a Christian in this New Testament sense of the word? Are you vitally, personally related to Christ by faith? Are you trusting in Him alone for eternal life? Or are you trusting in rules you've been trying to keep? trusting in your church membership? trusting in the fact that you are a citizen of a so-called "Christian" nation?

If you have been trusting in these false hopes, right this moment you can transfer your trust to Jesus Christ. He died for you on the cross. He spilled His blood to atone for your sins. He rose the third day from the dead so that you can have His resurrection life within you. Receive Him into your life as Savior and Lord. Receive His death on the cross and His resurrection from the grave as *in your stead*. At that moment you become a true Christian.

C.H. Koo was the eldest son in a very religious Korean family. While studying at Princeton University he met a Korean Christian girl. Her name was Soon. C.H. fell in love with Soon and wanted to marry her. But his father, a very committed Buddhist, would not give his consent.

C.H. wrote home to his parents again, asking them to reconsider. "Do you want me to be obedient and miserable the rest of my life," he asked, "or do you want me to be disobedient and happy?"

Finally his parents agreed that he could marry Soon on one condition: that she not go to church. Amazingly, Soon agreed! For nine years she lived without attending church. Then C.H. and Soon moved to Hong Kong. One day Soon encountered an American sitting on a park bench reading Billy Graham's book, *Angels.*

"You must be a Christian," Soon commented to the woman. "I am, too, but I never go to church because my husband's parents won't let me."

"Would they let you attend a Bible study in my home?" the woman wanted to know. Soon agreed to ask her husband. Before long she was attending the Bible study, and C.H. was playing basketball with the woman's husband. C.H. and Soon discovered that the Americans were missionaries in Hong Kong. On one of their meetings, the missionary couple invited C.H. and Soon to attend their church, where I was at that time the pastor.

C.H.'s uncle had recently died. The morning C.H. and Soon visited the church, my sermon was about Christ's resurrection and the Christian's hope beyond the grave.

Early that week, I took an Evangelism Explosion (EE) team to visit C.H. and Soon. C.H. was not ready to make a decision for Christ that evening, but several weeks later he telephoned to invite me to meet him for lunch.

"I want to be baptized!" he announced as we walked into the restaurant. I tried to make it clear that first he needed to trust Christ as his Savior. Right there in the restaurant I led him in the sinner's prayer. But Koreans can't pray softly. As C.H. prayed in a boisterous voice, the entire restaurant was focused on our table and listening!

C.H. was soundly converted. As he transferred his trust from religion to a relationship with Christ Jesus, his life was gloriously changed. Almost immediately he reflected the marks of a Christian. In fact, when he returned to Korea, his mother couldn't understand what had happened to her oldest son. The fact was he had experienced in his life . . .

2. The Miracle of a True Christian

C.H. was what the apostle Paul called "a new creation" (5:17). God had worked a miracle in his heart. Do you find it interesting that Paul uses the word *create* to express the change Christ produces in a new Christian? Creation is the greatest change possible. God created our beautiful universe by a spoken word! He took a world that was formless and empty (Genesis

1:2) and made it the beautiful planet on which we live. Paul uses that exact same imagery to describe the change that takes place when a person becomes a Christian. It is the miracle that takes place in the *heart*.

When C.H. Koo turned his life over to Christ, something miraculous happened. Some of the old things—a violent temper, nauseous pride, inordinate ambition—passed away. C.H. told me about his life before Christ. Occasionally he flew home to Korea to visit his parents. At dinner time the family would sit on the floor around a very low table. If C.H. didn't like the meal his mother had prepared, he would get to his feet and kick the food off the table! Now on his visits home he complimented his mother on her cooking and showed her respect and love.

C.H.'s language changed. His pride was replaced with genuine humility. His ambition for success in business became redirected to a deep ambition to obey and please the Lord. Everyone saw the miracle and knew that C.H. was a new creation.

Over and over I have seen that change. I saw it in Vietnam during my missionary service in that land. I saw it on Guam as I worked with Vietnamese refugees. I saw it in Hong Kong as I ministered at the Kowloon Tong Church. And I have seen it in my ministry in the United States. In fact, the change is perhaps a bit more dramatic when people come out of a totally non-Christian culture. I have seen people tear

down ancestral altars, destroy idols, burn fetishes, break enslaving habits. The only possible
explanation is re-creation: a miraculous change
of heart as Christ Jesus enters. They are new
creations. They are Christians in the New Testament sense of the word.

But that miracle within the human heart is
only half the story. A miracle takes place in
heaven as well. The sinner is reconciled to God:

> All this is from God, who reconciled us
> to himself through Christ and gave us the
> ministry of reconciliation: that God was
> reconciling the world to himself in Christ.
> (5:18-19)

While the miracle of creation takes place in
the believer's heart, the miracle of reconciliation takes place in heaven. The word *reconcile*
means to make friendly again, to settle the
quarrel, to restore peaceful harmony. How is
this a miracle for the Christian?

It's very simple. From the time Adam and
Eve, the first couple, fell into sin, there has
been a state of alienation between God and
humankind. From birth every person has
been at enmity with God. All of us were under God's wrath because of sin. But through
Christ and by faith in His death and resurrection, that unfriendly condition no longer
needs to exist. The very instant a person
trusts Christ for eternal life, he or she is no

longer at war with God. Instead of alienation there is peace and harmony. That, too, is a miracle!

The story is told about Themistocles, a Greek in the imperial palace of Macedon. Through a grave misdeed, Themistocles fell from the good graces of Emperor Philip. In fact, the emperor decided to have him executed. As the hapless man prepared to appear before the emperor for sentencing, he found young Prince Alexander playing in the courtyard. Scooping the little prince into his arms, the guilty Themistocles appeared before the emperor. When the vengeful emperor saw his smiling son in the arms of Themistocles, his wrath immediately abated. Instead of executing Themistocles, the emperor pardoned him.

That is an imperfect illustration of what happens in heaven when we condemned sinners receive God's Son into our lives. God sees not us but His Son. Because of Jesus, He pardons our sins and we are reconciled to the holy, righteous God. Instead of being our Judge, God becomes our loving heavenly Father.

But there is still another miracle when we receive Christ into our lives. Through faith in Christ we are made righteous. I call it the miracle of *history*.

God made him who had no sin to be sin for us, so that in him we might become the righteousness of God. (5:21)

The miracle of re-creation takes place in the heart and the miracle of reconciliation occurs in heaven. We might say that the miracle of being declared righteous in Christ takes place in history. Paul looks back to a point in time when Christ took upon Him the sins of the whole world. Because He bore our sins at that time in history, He now gives His righteousness to those who trust in Him. What a miracle that the perfect Son of God would take upon Himself the awful sins of a wicked world! What a miracle that we sinners can be declared righteous before an absolutely perfect and holy God!

Another miracle in history took place on the cross adjacent to the one Jesus occupied. A criminal, justly condemned to death, hung on that cross. Unable to do anything to save himself, he prayed a simple, sincere, one-sentence prayer: "Jesus, remember me when you come into your kingdom" (Luke 23:42).

Jesus replied, "I tell you the truth, today you will be with me in paradise" (23:43).

Throughout the ages of this Christian era, that same miracle has happened in the lives of millions of unrighteous, condemned sinners. They have found pardon through Jesus Christ and gained an eternal home in heaven.

This brings us to the third part of our definition of a Christian. Paul declares that because of such miraculous changes as we have just considered, "the old has gone, the new has come!" (2 Corinthians 5:17). Let's look at some of the *new* that comes to the person who is a true Christian. Let's call these new things . . .

3. The Marks of a True Christian

Without doubt, the true Christian is a marked person. Jesus likens him or her to "a city on a hill [that] cannot be hidden" (Matthew 5:14). In the first 16 verses of Second Corinthians 5, Paul suggests some very clear marks that identify the true Christian.

In these first 16 verses of Second Corinthians 5, I notice four marks that identify those who truly put their trust in Christ: a new *longing*, a new *labor*, a new *love* and a new *life*.

A New Longing

Now we know that if the earthly tent we live in is destroyed, we have a building from God, an eternal house in heaven, not built by human hands. Meanwhile we groan, longing to be clothed with our heavenly dwelling, because when we are clothed, we will not be found naked. For while we are in this tent, we groan and are burdened, because we do not wish to be unclothed but to be clothed with our heavenly dwelling, so that what is mortal may be swallowed up by life. Now it is God who has made us for this very purpose and has given us the Spirit as a deposit, guaranteeing what is to come.

> Therefore we are always confident and know that as long as we are at home in the body we are away from the Lord. . . . We are confident, I say, and would prefer to be away from the body and at home with the Lord. (5:1-8)

Isn't that amazing! Paul writes about death as something highly desirable. He says unequivocally that if he had a preference, he would leave his body and go home to be with the Lord! What confidence of life eternal! What assurance of existence beyond the grave!

I don't know any non-Christian who has this assurance. I don't know anyone outside of Christ who longs for his or her life to end so he or she can move into the hereafter.

In the year 1918 two young brothers, Le van Thai and Le van Long, listened outside a thatched chapel in Vietnam while missionaries Frank Irwin, D.I. Jeffrey and I.R. Stebbins—my dad—preached the gospel. Both brothers were antagonistic. At times they threw stones at my dad and the other two men. Or they tried to embarrass them with tough questions.

But the day finally came when, after struggling with their ancestor-worshiping background, they trusted Christ as their Savior. On July 4, 1920, my dad baptized both brothers, and they became strong pillars in the fledgling church. For more than 50 years, they served God as pastors. The younger of the two, Le van

Thai, was elected president of the national church in Vietnam.

In 1974, at the coastal city of Phan Rang, I had lunch with retired Pastor Le van Thai. By then many of his contemporaries, including his wife, had preceded him in death. Reminiscing through the years, he shared with me some fascinating stories. He concluded by telling me how much he wanted to leave this world. He said day and night he longed for heaven, where so many of his close associates were awaiting his arrival.

Rev. Le van Thai had to wait another 20 years. When I learned of his home-going, I couldn't help but think, *That which Brother Thai longed for has at last become reality! He's now in the place he wanted to be!*

One of the first marks evident in a true Christian is the new courage to face death, the new longing for heaven and home. But there is a second mark of a true Christian:

A New Labor

When people have a new heavenly home and a new eternal outlook, it affects their work. No longer are they working in order to gain merit or to get to heaven. They know they are saved by God's grace alone—not by works. But out of gratitude for their salvation they now work for their new Master. Their motive is to please their heavenly Lord. Notice how Paul describes it:

So we make it our goal to please him, whether we are at home in the body or away from it. For we must all appear before the judgment seat of Christ, that each one may receive what is due him for the things done while in the body, whether good or bad.

Since, then, we know what it is to fear the Lord, we try to persuade men. What we are is plain to God, and I hope it is also plain to your conscience. We are not trying to commend ourselves to you again, but are giving you an opportunity to take pride in us, so that you can answer those who take pride in what is seen rather than in what is in the heart. (5:9-12)

I like the way verse 9 reads in the King James Version: "Wherefore we labour, that, whether present or absent, we may be accepted of him." True Christians, according to Paul, because of their newfound faith, now labor for eternal values. Their motives have changed. Their goals are not the same. Their eyes are on the Lord. They want to please Him because they know that one day they will have to answer to their Lord.

Dang dang Khoa was a school teacher in the village of Bong Son, Vietnam. To support his rapidly growing family, he worked hard at his job. When he received Christ as his Savior, however, Dang dang Khoa's whole outlook in life changed. Now he taught with a zest and zeal he had not evidenced before. An eternal dimension took over his heart and mind. He seemed to do everything with an eye on eternity.

Finally he felt God was calling him to go to Bible school to learn to teach a new textbook—the Bible—in a new classroom—the church. I first met Khoa when he moved his large family to the village of Thach Ban to serve as student pastor for a small congregation of hardworking rice farmers. Shortly after he arrived there, I held evangelistic meetings at his church. Many new people were added to the congregation. Pastor Khoa worked tirelessly, faithfully visiting all the believers, preparing Sunday sermons. As might be expected under such an energetic pastor, the congregation continued to grow dramatically.

The people voted to build a larger church to accommodate all the people. Being poor rice farmers, they didn't have the financial means for such a noble project. There was no bank to give them a loan. What would they do? They decided to pool their funds and buy cement. The necessary sand needed for cement blocks they would hand carry from a nearby river. Wood for the rafters, doors and shutters they would cut in the forest and carry to the site.

As pastor-teacher, Khoa could easily have stood back and overseen the project. But, hard worker that he was, he joined his congregation in every step of the venture. One day I arrived unannounced at the building site. There I found Khoa dressed in black pajamas, barefooted, wearing a conical hat just like the rest of his people. He was carrying two large baskets of sand by means of a pole slung across his shoulders. Even more amazing, he had worked all the night before by moonlight!

What motivated Khoa to such unstinting labor? The answer is in the next mark of a true Christian:

A New Love

The world of Paul's day, like the world today, talked much about love. The Grecian and Roman gods were always in love. But it was a sensual love involving illicit sex and many gross practices contrary to God's Word. It was a love that was emotional, fleeting and totally dependent on the attractiveness of its object.

Hence a new word for love had to be found. Christians adopted the word *agape,* a love that finds its source in God alone. *Agape* love is not dependent upon the loveliness of its object. It is a love of the will, other-centered and sacrificial. It was—and is—a love difficult to explain. Some people thought Paul was crazy:

> If we are out of our mind, it is for the sake of God; if we are in our right mind, it is for you. For Christ's love compels us, because we are convinced that one died for all, and therefore all died. (5:13-14)

In effect Paul is saying, "I'm not crazy. I'm compelled—constrained—by the love of Christ." What did Paul do that the world thought crazy? He traveled to the ends of the Roman world with the gospel. Shipwrecked, imprisoned, stoned, beaten nearly to death, he kept going—and going—and going. No amount of persecution could slow his impassioned commitment to reach lost people for Christ.

Missionaries today are no different. Motivated by that same love, they make sacrifices that the world can't understand.

My sister and brother-in-law, Ruth and Ed Thompson, after more than 20 years of difficult missionary service in Cambodia, were not allowed by the government to continue. They had been working among Mnong tribespeople. Knowing there were Mnong across the border in Vietnam, they asked to be sent to Vietnam.

Well-meaning friends begged them not to go. "You'll die over there! The communists will kill you!" One woman even went so far as to pull some of the clothing out the shipping drum Ruth was packing.

"Ruth, you're crazy if you go to Vietnam!" the woman remonstrated. Quietly, calmly Ruth put the clothes back in the drum.

"I'm not crazy," she answered. "I'm constrained by the love of Christ. I must go, for Christ commands us to go." Ruth and Ed spent a year at Dalat learning Vietnamese.

Then they moved to Banmethuot. They expected to build a home in Quang Duc, a provincial capital and center of the Vietnam Mnong population.

They never moved to Quang Duc. During the 1968 Tet offensive, North Vietnamese troops attacked Banmethuot where Ruth and Ed were living. The communists killed Ed and Ruth and four other missionaries. Two others, taken captive, died later in the jungle.

Were those missionaries crazy? A non-Christian world would probably say so. But a Christian who has experienced God's *agape* love understands. They were compelled by the love of Christ.

A New Life

A true Christian is marked by a new longing, a new labor, a new love. He or she is also marked by a new life:

> [Christ] died for all, that those who live should no longer live for themselves but for him who died for them and was raised again.
> So from now on we regard no one from a worldly point of view. Though we once regarded Christ in this way, we do so no longer. (5:15-16)

Paul is saying that formerly he lived for himself with a worldly point of view. He was alive physically but dead spiritually. He was making a living, but not enjoying true life. As a branch severed from its trunk, he through sin had been separated from God. Dead in transgressions and sins (see Ephesians 2:1), he had been without hope until on the Damascus road he met Jesus Christ. But now, like a severed branch grafted back into the tree, Paul had been joined to Christ, the eternal Source of all true life. Now through a personal relationship with Christ, he had discovered a whole new life—life spelled with a capital *L*. Christ had promised new life to those who trust Him—eternal, abundant, meaningful, joyful life. It was a whole new quality of life. And Paul had found it.

That same new life in Christ is what the missionary offers wherever he or she goes. That's the mark that sets apart Christians in every land and culture. They may eat different food, wear different clothes and live in different styles of houses, but the same new life is evident. How beautiful, comforting, edifying, amazing is that new life!

Having experienced that kind of new life, the Christian wants to share it with others. He wants the whole world to find that same abundant, eternal Source. Thus motivated, he or she becomes involved in . . .

4. The Ministry of a True Christian

Christians have a great future in heaven. But Jesus saves them not just so they can enjoy heaven. He saves them to minister here on earth. True Christians understand what it means to be a Christian. They have experienced the threefold miracle of re-creation, reconciliation and righteousness. They are exhibiting this miracle through the four marks we have just discussed. It is time for them to become involved in God's twofold ministry for them. First, it is a ministry of *reconciling people to God*:

> [God] . . . gave us the ministry of reconciliation. . . . He has committed to us the message of reconciliation. (5:18-19)

Second, it is a ministry of *representing Christ to people*:

> We are therefore Christ's ambassadors, as though God were making his appeal through us. We implore you on Christ's behalf: Be reconciled to God. (5:20)

On many occasions I've seen this New Testament kind of Christian ministry overseas. Perhaps one of the most memorable was in a Koho tribal village, Datterday. Ten years earlier my eldest sister and her husband, Harriette and George Irwin, had taken the gospel for the first time to the people of that village. Conditions were deplorable. The homes were filthy and dilapidated. The villagers suffered from poverty and disease. The best farmland was devoted to tobacco. They used much of their rice for rice wine.

The people of Datterday did not name their children. They numbered them, but always starting with *two*. A number one child would be a prime target for the evil spirits they feared. Even so, the spirits were malevolent. Harriette was amazed to discover that in families giving birth to eight or 10 children, only one or two survived to adulthood.

"What happened to the others?" Harriette inquired.

"Oh, the spirits captured their souls."

To this benighted village George and Harriette brought the good news of a Savior who had given His life to reconcile them to God. Over and over George and Harriette repeated God's simple plan of salvation. They patiently answered the villagers' many questions. They visited the village not once but many times.

At last, one day, after consulting with the head men of the village, the chief announced that he and his people were ready to put their trust in Jesus Christ.

Ten years later Donna and I had opportunity to visit Datterday and see the results of that decision. We could hardly believe our eyes! It was just as Paul had said: The old had gone; the new had come.

The pastor stood at the village gate to greet us as we drove up. He led us to a longhouse where lunch had been prepared. After offering thanks to God, we feasted on barbecued venison, steamed mountain rice and deliciously cooked vegetables.

Following lunch, as we walked to the chapel, we noticed how clean the village was and how healthy and happy the children were. Disease and death seemed now the exception, not the rule. And many of the villagers were able to read and write.

"Who built this chapel?" I asked of the pastor.

"We did!" he said humbly but joyfully. "And it's all paid for! It's not very fancy, but it gives us a place to gather our people for worship, prayer and Bible study. Would you like to hear our children sing?"

I was amazed. Four-part harmony, three and four stanzas of each hymn, all from memory and without discord, in a primitive jungle setting. *Surely*, I thought, *this can't be the village Harriette described to me 10 years ago.*

It was and it was not.

It was the same village, but only after the power of the gospel had done its miraculous re-creating, reconciling. It was the same village, but now with genuine marks of new life, new love, new labor, new longing. Many of the people were the same people George and Harriette met 10 years earlier. But now they were demonstrating the fruits of a reconciling message and ministry.

What is a Christian? Visit Datterday and you will see there what you might see in myriad other villages on every continent of the world. The language, the skin color, the culture, the environment may be different. But there you will find the same personal relationship with Jesus Christ that bona fide Christians here in our land enjoy. You will see the same evidences of miraculous change that new Christians everywhere experience. You will recognize the same marks that set believers apart in our society. And you will be amazed to discover there a reconciling message and ministry equally effective and fruitful.

The supernatural impact of the gospel is what makes biblical missions so exciting and rewarding. It is so absolutely marvelous to see that "if anyone is in Christ, he is a new creation; the old has gone, the new has come!" *Anyone*—whatever the culture, the race, the strata of society, the educational level, the gender, the occupation—anyone can become a Christian in the New Testament sense of the term!

That's what biblical missions is about—making disciples who, like the early believers in Corinth, are truly Christian.

Study Guide Questions

1. How would you reply if someone were to ask you, "What is a Christian?"

2. When a person trusts Christ as Savior and enters into an eternal covenant with Him, what threefold miracle occurs?

3. Have you personally experienced this threefold miracle in your life?

4. What four marks should set apart a biblical Christian? Are these marks evident in your life? How do they show in your actions?

5. Name some things that Christians whom you know may be doing that non-Christians might consider "crazy."

6. How, exactly, did you become a Christian? Do people who rub shoulders with you every day know that you are a Christian? How can they tell?

7. Are you personally involved in a ministry of reconciliation? Describe it. If not, how might you become involved in such a ministry?

Chapter Four

Modern-Day Apostles

First Corinthians 9:1-18

"I F GOD CALLS YOU TO BE A MISSIONARY, don't stoop to become a king!" Some may feel this oft-quoted statement by Charles Haddon Spurgeon is a bit of hyperbole to which he succumbed in one of his more fanciful moments.

With all of his heart my missionary father believed the statement to be accurate. In the early 1940s he and the family set out by car to drive from New York to San Francisco. Alas! Our 1939 Buick broke down in Rawlins, Wyoming. By the time he had put his large family up in a motel for a week and paid for the major motor overhaul, Dad's already limited funds were dangerously low. When at last we reached the San Francisco Bay Bridge, Mom couldn't find enough coins to pay the toll.

To the great embarrassment of us children, she discovered in her purse some unused postage stamps. She counted out enough to satisfy the smiling toll collector, and we were on our way again. One of us dared to asked Dad if he didn't consider it pretty tough serving God as a missionary. Without hesitation Dad responded proudly, "We're not poor! We're rich. And I'm an ambassador of the King of kings and Lord of lords!"

That thought leads me to the thesis of this chapter: *To be a missionary in the New Testament sense is a high and holy calling.* But what exactly is a missionary in the New Testament sense of the word?

If you've read my earlier *Evangelism by the Book,* you may remember that one of my favorite Bible texts is First Corinthians 9. I want to look at it with you now. In First Corinthians 9 Paul defines for us what an apostle is. In that definition I believe he gives us insight into what a modern-day missionary should be. Paul shapes his job description around four key words that can be applied to the present-day missionary. One is the apostle's *work.* Another is his *wages.* The third is his *woe.* Finally, he remarks about his *witness.* Let's examine them in that order.

1. The Apostle-Missionary's Work

Notice the way Paul begins with a series of questions. All of the questions assume a Yes answer.

Am I not free? Am I not an apostle? Have I not seen Jesus our Lord? Are you not the result of my work in the Lord? Even though I may not be an apostle to others, surely I am to you! For you are the seal of my apostleship in the Lord. (9:1-2)

Paul was certifying to the church at Corinth that he was qualified by the Lord to be an apostle. Like the Corinthians themselves (see 9:19), he had been set free—liberated—by Christ Jesus. He had *seen* the Lord on the road to Damascus (Acts 9). The Lord had called and *sent* him from the midst of the Antioch assembly (Acts 13). Moreover, the very existence of these believers to whom he was writing was the *seal* of God's approval on his work.

Let's examine these qualifications as they relate to the missionary's work.

A Missionary Must Have Been Set Free

Sad, but true, some enter missionary service motivated by only an altruistic desire to help the less-advantaged or those in particularly difficult circumstances. They themselves have never been set free by Christ Jesus. They continue to bear their burden of sin.

They are able to offer temporal help to those among whom they work or to alleviate suffering and sickness. I have the highest admiration for those who turn their backs on homeland comforts and well-paying jobs in order to assist those in other lands who are in need. But they can never meet the deeper spiritual needs of the people to whom they go because their own spiritual needs have never been met. From an eternal standpoint, they are blind guides of the blind. And that leads into Paul's second point:

A Missionary Must Have "Seen" Jesus

Paul found his freedom in Jesus Christ as a result of seeing Him on the Damascus road. Then and there he surrendered totally, calling Jesus *Lord,* obeying His instructions. Three days later he was filled with the Holy Spirit and was baptized. The Bible says, "At once he began to preach in the synagogues that Jesus is the Son of God" (Acts 9:20).

Apostles were authoritative witnesses to the facts of the gospel and more especially to Christ's resurrection. Paul was not one of the original apostles. Some might have questioned his right to call himself an apostle. But on the Damascus road he encountered Jesus. It was a face-to-face encounter with his Lord, and it was life-changing. The persecutor became the preacher. Christ's number one enemy became one of His most faithful ministers.

In the same way a missionary is one whose life has been radically changed by a personal encounter with Jesus Christ. The best family upbringing and theological training cannot take the place of first hand faith in the Lord Jesus Christ.

A Missionary Must Be Sent

Evidently there were some in Corinth who

were questioning Paul's authority. Was he qualified to bring them the gospel? What right did he have to address the thorny issues troubling the church? As he writes, Paul defends his apostleship.

The term *apostle* simply means "one sent" or "a sent one." Over and over in his letters Paul points to the fact that God called him, that God sent him. And the church at Antioch confirmed that call. The elders "placed their hands" on Paul and his associate Barnabas and "sent them off" (Acts 13:3).

I realize that in the narrow sense of the term, apostles were a limited, special group of men. They had had personal contact with Jesus Christ in the flesh. Jesus selected them, appointing them to be the foundation stones of His church and the recorders of His revelation. But I'm also convinced that a broader application of the office might include many present-day missionaries. Especially is this so of those who, like the first-century apostles, are pioneering new frontiers for Christ. Whether you concur with me on that point, you will agree that missionaries, like apostles, are sent people.

Missionaries, to be effective in their work and to persevere amid difficulties, must know they have been sent by God. But, you ask, how do people know if God is truly sending them? I have studied the Scriptures minutely. I have talked with scores of divinely called missionaries. I know how it happened in my own personal experience. There are three basic factors: (1) Christ's so-called Great Commission. It is repeated in all the Gospels and the Acts. You cannot avoid it. (2) The application of Jesus' commission by the Holy Spirit's deep impression in your heart. (I will be saying more about this later on.) (3) The confirming of that "call" by the church's selecting, supporting and sending you.

Earlier I told you how God used evangelist Jack Wyrtzen, speaking from the words of the prophet Ezekiel, to apply the Great Commission to my heart. While still a student at Nyack College, church leaders regularly approached me. They said they wanted to send me as a missionary overseas. Even before I had my official interview with the sending board, word leaked out that they had appointed me for service in Vietnam.

Several months later, after the action was announced, church leaders laid their hands on me, commissioning me. I thought of how the church elders at Antioch had placed their hands on Paul and Barnabas and sent them off. For me it was a very meaningful experience.

For Donna, my wife, the details differed, but there were the same three elements.

Throughout the years those three factors—Christ's command, the Spirit's call and the church's commissioning—gave stability and confidence to us. They carried us triumphantly through the many vicissitudes of our life and ministry overseas.

Do you have a desire to serve God as an overseas missionary? I urge you to check that desire against these same three factors: Christ's command, the Spirit's personal call to you and the church's commissioning of you. You may have some very worthy motives for going. You may want to help people in need. You want to do something "really worthwhile" with your life. You want to give God the next two or five or 20 years of your life. But unless you are unquestionably "sent," you're in for a rough time when the discouragements come. (And they will.)

A Missionary Should Expect the Seal of Converts

I speak carefully, but with firm conviction. There are many instances, especially in pioneer areas, where one missionary "planted" the seed, another "watered" it and still others eventually reap the harvest (see 1 Corinthians 3:6). There are also resistant areas where, after years and years of labor, converts are extremely few. But we must be certain our lack of fruit is not the result of our lack of effort.

Recently a pastor friend told me of two missionaries who had visited his church to participate in a missions conference. He was chagrined to learn that one of the two had spent seven years in an animistic part of Indonesia without leading even one person to Christ! The missionary had spent all of his time studying the language and translating the Scriptures. He had not been trained to win people to Christ, and apparently he did not consider witnessing to people his responsibility!

The second missionary had spent 17 years in the Caribbean without leading a single person to Jesus Christ. Worse, he didn't know how! Yet he had been training pastors to serve the Lord. He was reproducing "after his kind" a host of pastors who also did not have a clue as to how to lead someone to Christ.

There are missionaries on every continent who, when asked their concept of missionary work, would respond similarly. "My work is meeting airplanes and securing travel documents." "I keep the mission's financial records and answer the telephone." "I build houses for missionaries; I construct churches, camp grounds and medical clinics."

I am not denigrating any of these things. They are tasks that someone must do. When I was a missionary in Vietnam, I depended upon such support people. But bussing people to airports and bookkeeping and building are not enough! God selects, summons and sends us to impact *people,* and to impact them for eternity. Christ sent His followers to make disciples.

When I moved to Omaha in 1980, I met a shy young missionary candidate from a small farming community in Alabama. For her pre-appointment "home service," she was serving as a secretary at Christ Community Church.

I inquired of Regene what she would be doing later when she went to Brazil. She said she would be working in the mission office as a bookkeeper-secretary. I asked her if I might train her to win people to Christ. I wanted to show her how to make disciples and to train those disciples to win others.

I watched as a diffident office secretary gradually became a confident one-on-one evangelist. Today Regene is serving in Sao Paulo as a bookkeeper-secretary—during the day. In the evenings she has been training pastors, church leaders and lay Christians to obey the Great Commission. She has been impacting all kinds of people for eternity. If you were to ask her what her work is, I'm sure she would not reply in terms of her daytime duties. She would say, "It's winning Brazilians—moms, dads, youth and children—to Christ. It's discipling them and training them to win others."

Missions and churches send out missionaries without instilling in them a proper sense of what their work really is. In so doing, they do the worker a great disservice. And they are not being fair with the people who support these missionaries. They are not being faithful to Christ and to His last command to go and make disciples. These missions and churches should require—and provide—adequate hands-on training for their candidates. Then when they arrive at their tasks they will impact people for eternity, just as Christ intends for them to.

2. The Apostle-Missionary's Wages

A second key word Paul uses to describe the apostle-missionary has to do with his compensation. When I first read and re-read the next verses of First Corinthians 9, I thought them uninteresting and not too instructive. But like many other Scriptures, as I took time to reflect and meditate on these verses, they became both practical and relevant.

> Don't we have the right to food and drink? Don't we have the right to take a believing wife along with us, as do the other apostles and the Lord's brothers and Cephas? Or is it only I and Barnabas who must work for a living? (9:4-6)

Paul has been writing the Corinthians concerning the eating of certain foods (see chapter 8). Now Paul addresses his rights in the matter of support by the Corinthian church. He does so in four areas: *maintenance, marriage, making tents* and *mission versus church support.*

Maintenance

It was accepted in New Testament times that apostles should be maintained by those *to whom* or *in whose behalf* they ministered. Hence, Paul's question: "Don't we have the right to food and drink?"

He appeals to others in a similar service category: to soldiers, who are given wages; to the vineyard worker, who is free to eat of the grapes; to the goatherd who derives his sustenance from the flock he tends. And so Paul concludes: "If we have sown spiritual seed among you, is it too much if we reap a material harvest from you? If others have this right of support from you, shouldn't we have it all the more?"

This principle of maintenance can be applied to every age and culture. Churches are obligated to support their spiritual leaders. When the pioneer missionaries launched God's work in Vietnam, they taught the first Christians to support their pastors. When in 1975 we missionaries had to leave, the church survived and has increased. The church was established on the Rock Christ Jesus. It was early taught biblical principles of self-support.

Marriage

Paul asks, "Don't we have the right to take a believing wife along with us?" (9:5). The answer? "Of course, you have that right!

In 1918, when my parents first set out for Vietnam, missionaries were sent to the field single. The rationale behind such an odd policy was to insure the sending church that all its missionaries were clearly called and highly motivated. Two years after their arrival in Vietnam, my parents were married.

But times have changed. While mission boards are just as concerned as ever that both husband and wife are called and motivated, they usually leave the matter of marriage up to the missionary couple.

As a college freshman, I became engaged to my high school sweetheart. She was studying at Moody Bible Institute; I was at Nyack College. Shortly after our engagement, my fiancee suggested we should stay in the States and perhaps seek teaching positions at Hampden DuBose Academy, the secondary school we both had attended. Sensing that her commitment for missions was not as strong as mine, I reluctantly broke our engagement.

Four months later I started dating a Nyack sophomore, Donna Stadsklev. She had been born in Côte d'Ivoire, West Africa, to pioneer missionaries. She was firmly committed to missionary service in Africa. A year later our relationship became more and more serious, and an obvious question began to surface: In which country would we serve?

When furloughing missionaries asked us that question, I would reply facetiously, "Donna will serve in Africa while I am in Vietnam. Then we'll meet on furlough!" Or, "We'll live in India so she can commute to Africa while I commute to Vietnam!"

Finally, in January, 1954, I drove to Canada where Donna was taking a one-year missionary nursing course. Late one evening I parked at the edge of a cliff in Toronto and told Donna to choose between the cliff and me. Donna chose me and even agreed to spend the rest of her life with me in Vietnam.

Marrying Donna was the second most important decision of my life—second only to asking Christ to be my Savior and Lord. No two people could have lived together more compatibly. I could write another book about our blissful life together. But since this book is about missions, let me add just one emphatic word here: *Your selection of a spouse is crucial. The person you marry will make you or break you.*

Making tents

Having remarked on the subjects of maintenance and marriage, Paul goes on to speak about how he supported himself by making tents. "Is it only I and Barnabas who must work for a living?" Paul asks (9:6).

Taking Paul's cue, there is today a sizable movement toward what is commonly called *tentmaker* missionaries. These are teachers, engineers, business people who find employment within their profession and serve the cause of missions along with their other work. Unlike other missionaries, they are not dependent on the gifts of supporting churches. In some cases, they may be the *only* expatriate Christian evangelists and church planters in a country. The fact that they are ordinary working people may make it easier for people to relate to them.

We admire these who, like Paul, support themselves in order to "offer [the gospel] free of charge." Were it not for these, some countries would have *no* personal gospel witness. There are, however, practical reasons for missionaries' receiving their financial support from homeland churches.

Not all nations of the world are happy to see expatriates gobble up scarce jobs that their own citizens need for livelihood. Frequently the only job openings for expatriates are in highly specialized fields where most missionaries would not qualify. Then, too, tentmakers, however highly motivated, must divide their loyalty between their secular work and their missionary work. They cannot devote full time and energy to the work of God's kingdom.

There is also the practical matter of prayer backing. Remember Jesus' words? "Where your treasure is, there your heart will be also" (Matthew 6:21). Jesus was urging people to store their treasures in heaven, not on earth. But the principle He enunciated is universal. Our interest tends to focus on wherever our money is. If we have a financial stake in an overseas missionary, we will more likely pray for that missionary. We will take a much more active interest in the work he or she is doing.

Mission Support

By "mission support" I refer to support of missionaries from or through the sending church or mission. If you have digested Paul's argument in 9:7-14 concerning "rights," you probably have a question: "Logic may be on the side of missionary support from the sending church. But does not Paul argue that the evangelist should be supported by the people evangelized? Paul says, 'If we have sown spiritual seed among you, is it too much if we reap a material harvest from you?' Why should the sending church continue to bear this heavy burden?"

Paul indeed amassed biblical precedent for support from the receiving churches. But he also provides us with a good answer to the question and a reasonable guiding principle:

> But we did not use this right. On the contrary, we put up with anything rather than hinder the gospel of Christ. . . .
> I have not used any of these rights. . . . What then is my reward? Just this: that in preaching the gospel I may offer it free of charge. . . . (9:12, 15, 18)

Paul sensed that if in Corinth he exercised his right to support, it would become a stumbling block. Believers and unbelievers might misunderstand his motive for preaching the gospel. They might think he was doing it for personal gain. Rather than to risk hindering the gospel, he supported himself as a tentmaker missionary.

For those same reasons, present-day mission-aries, if not supported by their sending churches, support themselves as "tentmakers." Then, ideally and in keeping with biblically sound principles, they teach the receiving churches to support their own pastors and the church's own missionary outreach.

3. The Apostle-Missionary's Woe

We come now to the third part of the apostle/missionary's job description. I call it his *woe*. Paul states it clearly:

> When I preach the gospel, I cannot boast, for I am compelled to preach. Woe to me if I do not preach the gospel! If I preach voluntarily, I have a reward; if not voluntarily, I am simply discharging the trust committed to me. (9:16-17)

Paul is not saying he will be punished if he doesn't preach the gospel. Rather, he is couching in forceful language the responsibility that he understands and deeply feels. Some undefined disaster might rightfully come to him if he does not proclaim such wonderful news. Paul had been divinely commissioned (and we have been, too) to announce the good news of life through Jesus Christ!

There is a story of a large band of travelers making a long and weary trek across a vast desert. Having passed no oasis, their supply of drinking water was running dangerously low. In desperation they divided the strongest into small groups, each facing a different direction of the compass. From each group they sent the strongest ahead, one in advance of the next. The instructions were simple: Should anyone discover water, he was to relay the word back down the line.

As the lines of communication stretched farther and farther across the desert, like spokes from a hub, one of the leaders came upon a water spring.

"Water!" he shouted. And the man behind him repeated the good news. And so by that relay, all got the welcome word. Just in time they had ample water, without which they would have perished.

Mark, the evangelist, relates a similar event. You will find it in chapter 16 of his Gospel. For three days Jesus' disciples had mourned the death of their Master. Their outlook seemed hopeless. They were filled with despair.

Then early on Sunday morning, a small band of women brought spices to the grave to anoint Jesus' body. Arriving at the tomb, they discovered that the large, very heavy stone sealing the grave had been moved aside. What appeared to them to be a young man dressed in white announced, "You are looking for Jesus the Nazarene, who was crucified. He has risen! He is not here. . . . Go, tell his disciples . . ." (Mark 16:6-7).

Like the desert travelers who knew life-sustaining water was at hand, the women relayed the good news. And ever since, the followers of Jesus have been relaying the joyful message of a risen, triumphant Savior.

The question for us today is this: Will we continue to pass on that good news to yet others who still are dying without hope?

4. The Apostle-Missionary's Witness

The missionary, then, is first and foremost an announcer of good news. He or she may be a teacher, a doctor, an aviator, a linguist. But he or she is much more. The good news he or she proclaims is the best and most important news this world can possibly hear!

It is my conviction that every missionary, no matter what his or her particular specialty, should be a bearer of the good news of Jesus Christ. Many missionaries serve in supporting roles: secretaries, mechanics, translators, pilots, business managers, school teachers, builders. Because of the nature of their work, some of these tend to think the Lord doesn't expect them to deliberately, strategically share the gospel. Nothing could be farther from the truth!

If here in the homeland every believer is to be a witness (and that is the biblical standard), then certainly support missionaries should be adequately equipped and totally committed to passing on this saving truth of Jesus Christ to those who do not know Him. If they are not conversant in the local language, they will find expatriates with whom they can share the gospel.

At Christ Community Church we will not support or send anyone as a missionary unless he or she has been trained to share Christ and is a proven witness here at home. Before our youth are sent on short-term mission trips, they must be trained in Evangelism Explosion (EE). And believe me, it is exciting when our missionaries—adults and youth—return from abroad. It is exciting to hear their reports of how God has used them to relay to others the same gospel that Paul felt a "woe" to proclaim.

I am writing these particular lines on the Pacific island of Fiji. A team of 16 lay people and 4 pastors from our church has ministered this past week on two different islands. We gave EE training to 58 islander pastors and lay leaders. We saw 143 people come to faith in Christ. One of the local pastors, trained in Canada, said he had pastored here for nearly two years with no evident fruit. Yet when equipped at the EE Leadership Clinic, he began to see people turning to Christ on every hand. If pastors and lay people, speaking in their mother tongue, can effectively, fruitfully proclaim the good news like this, cannot so-called support missionaries do the same? It's a matter of motivation, accountability and equipping.

But the apostle Paul was not satisfied to merely *proclaim* the good news, thrilling though that experience may be. He wanted to see people *won to Christ*—as many people as possible! Sense Paul's driving passion as he writes:

> Though I am free and belong to no man, I make myself a slave to everyone, to win as many as possible. To the Jews I became like a Jew, to win the Jews. To those under the law I became like one under the law (though I myself am not under the law), so as to win those under the law. To those not having the law I became like one not having the law (though I am not free from God's law but am under Christ's law), so as to win those not having the law. To the weak I became weak, to win the weak. I have become all things to all men so that by all possible means I might save some. I do all this for the sake of the gospel, that I may share in its blessings. (9:19-23)

A few sentences later Paul likens his ministry to a foot race and to a boxing match. In both contests, the participants do everything possible to win. But Paul's consuming passion is not a foot race or a boxing match. He strives to win people to Christ!

There is a well established rule among salespeople, diplomats, politicians and even preachers. If you want to win someone over to your point of view or the product you are selling, *you must first win the person to yourself.* It is so in sharing the good news of Jesus Christ. Before you can effectively win someone to your Savior, you must gain the other's confidence. By the grace of God and in the power of the Holy Spirit, you must gain the right to be heard.

In order to achieve this worthy goal, Paul seems to suggest four important steps. To make them easier for you to remember, I'll call these steps *posture, penetration, preparation* and *prize.* We'll be looking at them in the next chapter— chapter 5. It's an exciting discussion of what it really means to be a missionary at the turn of the 21st century.

Study Guide Questions

1. According to Paul's use of the word *apostle,* in what ways does the present-day missionary resemble a New Testament apostle?

2. If missionaries are to be sure they qualify as "sent ones," what three factors need to line up?

3. Paul said there was a seal that attested to his apostleship as one sent by God. What was that seal?

4. In First Corinthians 9, what does Paul declare to be his true and lasting work? What might we say should be the real work of today's missionary?

5. According to our study of First Corinthians 9, do you think it is biblical and healthy for a sending church to give financial support to indigenous pastors in the countries where the church's missionaries serve? Why or why not?

6. In the case of couples entering missionary service, how important is it for both husband and wife to sense God's call? Explain.

7. Should missionaries expect financial support from the national Christians among whom they serve? Explain your answer.

8. Do you agree that it is important for *all* missionaries—including support personnel—to be able to effectively, winsomely, fruitfully share the gospel? Why?

Chapter Five

Missionaries Who Win

First Corinthians 9:19-27

THE VIETNAMESE HAVE A SAYING, "When you enter a family's home, you follow its customs, just as when you enter a river you follow its bends." Those words were indelibly impressed on my mind as Pastor Nguyen van Thin and I entered a Vietnamese village in Phu Yen Province for my first evangelistic thrust.

As our first order of business, we went to the office of the village chief to obtain his permission for open-air meetings. The chief seemed uncharacteristically abrupt. He looked at me coldly. I feared Pastor Thin and I were in for a rough time of it.

But then I greeted the chief—in his language and properly. Suddenly his whole demeanor changed. Not only did he give us the needed permit, but he seemed ready to give us anything else we might have asked for! The villagers were equally responsive, listening to every word of the music and message. They seemed reluctant to see our meeting end. Why? Because I, a foreigner, had taken the trouble to learn their language. I had "followed the bends" of their river.

Before you can win people to a hearing of the gospel, you must win them to yourself as a person. For the missionary, it's the difference between success and failure, fruit and no fruit, winning and losing.

Having looked in Chapter 4 at the missionary's work, wages, woe and witness, we now look at him or her as a person. In First Corinthians 9:17-27, Paul sets out four steps to being an effective proclaimer of the gospel. Here they are: *positioning, penetration, preparation* and *prize.*

The Missionary's Positioning

Real estate people have an oft-quoted maxim. To sell a house three things are important: location, location and location. In life and in business, positioning is everything! Our relationship to others with whom we live and work makes all the difference.

If that is true, exactly how does the apostle Paul position himself? In 9:19 he declares unequivocally,

> Though I am free and belong to no man, I make myself a slave to everyone, to win as many as possible.

In effect Paul is saying, "In order to have maximum impact for God and win a maximum number of people to Christ, I take the position of a bond servant. No one forces me into this position. I take it voluntarily." Paul's positioning sounds remarkably like that of Christ Jesus,

> Who, being in very nature God,
>> did not consider equality with God
>> something to be grasped,
> but made himself nothing,
>> taking the very nature of a servant.
> (Philippians 2:6-7)

In Paul's day, what exactly did it mean to be a bond servant, a slave? And how specifically might a missionary voluntarily assume such a position?

Self-denial

Slaves belonged to their master. They were forced to live selfless lives. The first and perhaps most important step in becoming a missionary whom God can use is to die to self. Such a death is not a once-for-all act. Missionaries must die daily in every area of their lives and ministry.

I first understood and experienced this death principle as a sophomore in college. I wrestled in my heart with issues such as pride, lust, self-centeredness, worldly ambition. I saw that these things were sinful and displeasing to God. They ran counter to His will for my life.

They grieved His Spirit. They were impediments to my growth in Christlikeness. Dying to these things was painful! I wept so copiously that the floor under the chair where I knelt became a pool of water.

Many times subsequently God has revealed other areas of my life to which I have had to die. By faith I have reckoned them dead also. I have had to die to personal goals, to selfish ambitions, to earthly comforts. I have had to die to natural desires, to physical well-being.

Our departure by ship back in 1957 for Vietnam was painful. It was not easy to say goodbye to family, friends and the comforts of America. And certainly I was not looking forward to the inevitable seasickness ahead of me. But the more I died daily to self, the more I experienced God's resurrection life and power working through me for His glory and purposes. The more I died daily to self, the more freedom I found to serve the Vietnamese people I was longing to win to Christ.

Serving

A slave's life was primarily one of serving. And missionaries, if they are missionaries "by the Book," will be like Jesus, who came not to be served, "but to serve, and to give his life as a ransom for many" (Mark 10:45).

One of my first missionary tasks was driving Pastor Nguyen van Thin and other national workers out into the villages to conduct evangelistic meetings. For several months my duties were limited to driving my jeep and playing my trombone. I confess I was tempted to complain. Had I come all the way to Vietnam just to be a chauffeur and to play a trombone? But as my language ability increased, these men invited me to give flannelgraph Bible lessons to the children. And after two years in Vietnam, I began to preach!

But my role as servant did not end at that point. Nor did it ever end. Not even when I became field director! I learned an important lesson through all that service. Servanthood was the route to wholehearted acceptance, both by my fellow missionaries and the Vietnamese. It was a certain route to winning.

Sacrificing

A slave's entire life was one of sacrifice. Bond servants sacrificed materially, physically, socially and in nearly every other way. As missionaries in Vietnam, possibly one of the most difficult sacrifices was our personal privacy. Americans place great value on privacy. For Vietnamese, privacy was not an important value. It just wasn't a part of their culture. Very early in our missionary careers, Donna and I had "opportunity" to sacrifice our privacy. After a year of language study in Danang, we were assigned to Tuy Hoa, the seat of Phu Yen Province. Until then, no missionary had lived anywhere in Phu Yen Province.

I rented a truck (including a driver), packed all our furniture and household goods into it and started south. One of my missionary colleagues, Robert Henry, went with me. Arriving midday at Tuy Hoa, we told the driver to park the truck while the two of us went in search of a place to live. Since all the French villas had been destroyed during the war between the French and the Vietminh, there was nothing available except a store. We rented it on the spot. And by nightfall we were moved in.

When Donna arrived the next day, she discovered that this best possible residence in town had absolutely no privacy. The building had no windows. For light and air, we had to leave two panels of the front door open. We bought a folding screen to prevent passersby from looking directly into our living-dining area. But it was a lost cause. We were the only Americans in the whole province, and the villagers had little else to do except observe us. Children discovered that by using a long stick they could pull aside the fabric on the folding screen and thus have a good view of our meal times.

Behind us was a Chinese/Vietnamese school. To the right, a hall where young people played table tennis. Across the street, the local theater. In Vietnam, school children recite their lessons at the top of their voices. We listened to that all day. By the time school closed, the clatter of table tennis had taken over, joined soon by the loudspeakers from the theater across the street, blasting forth unbelievably loud music.

Even after our Mission built us a more comfortable house on the quiet, cool edge of town, we had but minimal privacy. There were the ever-present household helpers. And a multitude of visitors at every hour of the day. We shared meals with the visitors. At night they often slept in our chairs and even on the dining room table.

Out in the villages where we traveled for ministry, personal privacy was even at greater premium. I would wait until dark to shower. I shaved with a gathering of children watching. When Donna and our children traveled with me, women would pull up Donna's blouse to see if she was pregnant. Seeing she was not, they wanted to know her secret for not giving birth every year.

How did we react to this invasion of our privacy? First, we had to recognize the differences in Vietnamese culture and ours. Then we had to ask God to give us grace, as bond servants, to see that personal privacy was something we must joyfully sacrifice for the sake of the gospel.

Suffering

Few understood suffering like slaves understood it. Whether privation, overwork, beatings or other maltreatment, their lot in life was hard.

Most missionaries find the first term of service the most difficult. There are the cultural adjustments I have already alluded to. The food is different. There are a multitude of bacteria that Westerners have little or no resistance to. I have already mentioned the malaria and boils that plagued me my first term and Donna's bone infection that came close to taking her life.

How do missionaries respond to such testings? Do they lose faith in God? A few possibly do. Do they pack up and head home? Some do—some of necessity. Most are able to ask God for grace to go on serving joyfully as bond servants of the Master who called them. That doesn't mean they aren't tempted to quit. It doesn't mean they have no second thoughts. After all, missionaries are human. But they see themselves as slaves of Jesus Christ. They take the attitude He modeled. And by God's grace and power and to His glory they become winners.

2. The Missionary's Penetration

Next Paul writes to the Corinthians about his penetration of their multifaceted culture. He writes about his identification with them, his acculturation. Again, we face those "bends of the river." Our American stock phrase for it: "When in Rome, do as the Romans." Paul makes these comments as he reviews his ministry in Corinth:

To the Jews I became like a Jew, to win the Jews. To those under the law I became like one under the law (though I myself am not under the law), so as to win those under the law. To those not having the law I became like one not having the law . . . so as to win those not having the law. To the weak I became weak, to win the weak. I have become all things to all men so that by all possible means I might save some. (9:20-22)

Two thoughts stand out for me as I examine those verses and review my own missionary ministry: the opposites we encounter and the flexibility that must characterize our response.

Opposites

In his missionary journeys Paul encountered people who were different: different from him and different from people elsewhere. There were Jews and Gentiles. Among the Gentiles there were the educated Greeks and the still barbarian pagans. He encountered those who were eager to receive the gospel. He encountered others whose only interest seemed to be fleshly pursuits. To all he sought to minister the gospel without first attempting to alter their customs and culture.

Donna and I were hardly off the ship in Saigon in 1957 when we started to note the differences between rural Vietnamese culture and our own. At our first church service, we discovered that men and women sat on opposite sides of the sanctuary. Back in 1957, women in America customarily wore hats to Sunday morning church. In Vietnam the women were bareheaded and the men wore black turbans!

American etiquette dictated that men should open doors for women and allow women to enter first. In Vietnam the man always entered first and the woman respectfully followed. At first Donna did not appreciate this difference until she realized, in the country areas, that *I* first encountered the spider webs! When I led the way down a path, I was first to meet a tiger or step on a Vietcong land mine!

And so it went. At funerals, the mourners wore white, not black. Vietnamese celebrate the anniversaries of death rather than birth. Women peel vegetables by pushing the knife away from them. If they serve pie, the point is positioned away from the eater.

One day in Hue I was pulling on the oars of a row boat. As I crooked my neck to look across the river, I noticed that Vietnamese rowers were pushing their oars. They were facing forward and could easily see where they were going! Suddenly I realized that it wasn't a matter of who was right or wrong; it was just different. It was important for me, in the Vietnamese culture, to follow the Vietnamese pattern. This called for adjustment on my part. It called for . . .

Flexibility

When Paul said that he became all things to

all men, he certainly was setting a standard of flexibility for himself. And as you read through the book of Acts and the Letters written by Paul, you can observe that flexibility in his preaching, his writing, his leadership and, above all else, his lifestyle. But how does that carry over into missionary life and ministry?

We Americans tend to be pretty direct in everything we do and say. Just the opposite is true generally in the Orient. For example, if Donna needed a cup of sugar for the cake she was baking, it would not do to run to the neighbor and ask to borrow a cup of sugar. Instead, she would pay a social visit to the neighbor. After 30 minutes of general conversation, Donna might casually mention that she was baking a cake. Her hope would be that the neighbor would ask if she had everything for it she needed. If the neighbor did not ask, Donna might mention how forgetful she was the last time she went to market in not thinking to buy sugar. And if *that* hint failed to elicit the desired response, Donna might say just as she was getting ready to leave, "Oh, yes, would you have a cup of sugar you could lend me until I go to market tomorrow?"

How flexible the missionary can be in all these cultural differences determines whether he or she will be a winner or a loser.

3. The Missionary's Preparation

Paul next turns to the illustration of a foot

race and the kind of training it takes to produce a winner:

> Do you not know that in a race all the runners run, but only one gets the prize? Run in such a way as to get the prize. Everyone who competes in the games goes into strict training. (9:24-25)

Training for Paul's missionary work is at least as strict. The apostle adds:

> I beat my body and make it my slave so that after I have preached to others, I myself will not be disqualified for the prize. (9:27)

Paul was saying that if athletes need to train rigorously, how much more do those who want to become winners in ministry need to train. For today's missionaries, that begins with their . . .

Formal Education

Some prospective missionaries, anxious to get overseas as soon as possible, look for sending organizations with the lowest academic requirements. I heard of one fellow who remarked, "I've got my Bible and the Holy Spirit. What more do I need?" Experience has proven over and over that a sound education in liberal arts and theology, along with basic courses in missiology, go a long way toward making a winning missionary.

Personally, I was stimulated by the examples of Moses, Jesus and Paul to get the best possible education. At that time I thought I would be spending most of my years evangelizing rural peasants. Little did I realize that my overseas service would also include being field director for what was then the largest staff in the Alliance. In Hong Kong I had 10 or more regulars in my Sunday congregation with earned doctorates. In my work with Evangelism Explosion I have trained pastors and church leaders around the globe. I am writing books on evangelism, discipleship and missions. My counsel to you, if you sense God's call to missionary service: *Don't limit your potential by short cuts. Get the best education possible.*

Home Service

My church, The Christian and Missionary Alliance, requires of its missionary candidates a minimum of two years in homeland service. Prospective missionaries, in their haste to get overseas, sometimes shy away from this additional time of preparation. But missionaries who have this practical testing are much more likely to stick it out when the going gets rough. They are and end up winners.

Language and Cultural Study

I lump these two categories together because in practice they are quite inseparable. One of the best ways to learn a culture is to learn that culture's language.

Before leaving for overseas, I took courses and read everything I could get my hands on that dealt with linguistics and culture. One small book, relatively old and probably out of print by now, set forth two principles for language learning that proved helpful to me. (I regret that I do not recall even the book's title.) The author suggested that children learn to speak a language quickly and accurately because they learn in exact reverse from the way most adults learn. Adults first learn to read and write a new language, then to speak and finally to hear with understanding. Children begin by listening for a couple of years. Then they speak simple words, then phrases and gradually full sentences. *After that* they learn to read and write.

The author's second point was the importance of oral drill and repetition of phrases and full sentences. Psychologists say it takes the average person 28 repeats to fix something permanently in his or her mind. Moreover, children learn to speak in complete phrases or sentences, not word-by-word. Hence their flow of speech becomes smooth as they think of and add each individual word.

Arriving on the field, I determined there would be no shortcuts. From day one I immersed myself in studying Vietnamese and Vietnamese culture. I looked for every opportunity to hear the spoken language: on the radio, in the barber shop and other shops around town, in people's homes and especially in church.

Vietnamese is monosyllabic, meaning the words are just one syllable in length. Unlike Chinese, it is written in the Roman script. Easy, you say. But Vietnamese is also a tonal language. Each of those one syllable words can mean two to five different things, depending on the inflection you give it. For example, the word *ma* can mean "devil," "mother," "but," "horse" or "rice shoot," depending on the inflection. So you see the problem. You might inadvertently call your mother a horse or a rice shoot or even a devil! The opportunities for error are mind-boggling.

Language learning probably is at once the most difficult and the most crucial step in missionaries' preparation for cross-cultural ministry. More than anything else, fluency in the language determines their effectiveness as witnesses of the good news. Make the extra effort to learn the language well and you will find unbelievable doors of opportunity open before you.

4. The Missionary's Prize

As Paul continues in his analogy of the race and the runner, he writes about the prize that highly motivated him in his missionary journey to Corinth. I will repeat a couple of the verses we have already looked at:

Do you not know that in a race all the runners run, but only one gets the prize? Run in such a way as to get the prize. Everyone who competes in the games goes into strict training. They do it to get a crown that will not last; but we do it to get a crown that will last forever. Therefore I do not run like a man running aimlessly; I do not fight like a man beating the air. No, I beat my body and make it my slave so that after I have preached to others, I myself will not be disqualified for the prize. (9:24-27)

Paul says he was drawn and driven by a desire to win the prize. He then contrasts two kinds of prizes: crowns that last forever and crowns that don't.

Temporal Crowns

The crowns awarded the winners of the Isthmian Games of Paul's day were pine or palm wreaths that they wore when they returned home from the contests. At first the crowns brought great glory to the winners. Shortly, however, they wilted, losing any semblance of attractiveness. As I look back over my 20 years of missionary service in Vietnam, I have much to praise God for. But I also have some regrets. One of my deepest regrets concerns the large amount of time I invested in an effort to win temporal "crowns"—those pursuits and objects that become useless or meaningless with the passing of time.

Here's an example. While serving for three years in Hue, I spent an excessive amount of time and effort remodeling the youth center where we lived. I painted shutters, reconstructed the fence, rearranged rooms and beautified the grounds. Those things had their value, of course. But they were hardly top priority in light of the limited time I had to invest in the youth at the center. As I look back, I can see that I should have concentrated much more on personal evangelism. I should have been discipling new believers. I should have been equipping the Christian youth for ministry. Had I done so, there would be today much more lasting fruit.

In 1994 Donna and I celebrated our 40th anniversary with a two-week trip back to Vietnam. We had opportunity to see our youth center in Hue. The communist government, having no use for a Christian youth center, is using it for an office. As I viewed (and photographed) the facility I had spent so much time remodeling, my heart ached. I had done all of it with the best of intentions. But I had invested too much time in brickwork and paint and too little in the young people. Remorse gripped me as I thought of the scores of youth I might have more prudently given my attention to.

I must not leave you with the impression

that no youth in those years were won to Christ, discipled and equipped. But I do want to confess that if I had my life to live over, I would work less for the temporal crowns that pass away.

There are many things in which missionaries can invest time and energy: books, organizations, schools, hospitals, chapels. The list goes on and on. They are all good, but they are only means toward the real prize. The real prize is people.

Eternal Crowns

And what was Paul's eternal crown? I can think of only two things in this life that are eternal. One is the Word of the Lord, which "stands forever" (1 Peter 1:25). The other? Never-dying people who will spend eternity either in heaven or hell. It seems logical to suppose that the "crown" Paul was striving to win was made up of the people of Corinth and other places where he ministered. In First Corinthians 9:1-2 he asks: "Are you not the result of my work in the Lord? Even though I may not be an apostle to others, surely I am to you! For you are the seal of my apostleship in the Lord." *They* were the ones for whom he made himself a slave to win (9:19). They were the ones for whom he became weak to win (9:22).

This interpretation was confirmed for me when I read what Paul wrote to the church in Thessalonica. He asks, "What is our hope, our joy, or the crown in which we will glory in the presence of our Lord Jesus when he comes? Is it not you? Indeed, you are our glory and joy" (1 Thessalonians 2:19-20).

When on April 30, 1975, I was forced to leave Vietnam, I left behind a number of things that will ultimately disintegrate. There were most of my books. There was a Ford van that I had worked hard to equip for evangelistic campaigns. There were various mementos and keepsakes. I may never see those perishable things again. But the people whom I was able to win, to disciple, to equip for ministry—they are eternal. They are my comfort and joy. I will meet them again in eternity around God's throne!

During the visit Donna and I made to Vietnam, we had the joy of meeting one of the approximately 10 young people we had discipled during our time in Hue. I shall not give his full name lest doing so endanger his life. But both Donna and I had spent time with Dinh, teaching him God's Word and training him in personal evangelism. We had counseled him regarding his walk with God. We had prayed with him and encouraged him during his times of trial and temptation. We had even sponsored Dinh's study in Bible school so he could train for full-time Christian work.

Now, a score of years later, we had the indescribable joy of meeting him again. We met his wife as well, and his children. He told us about his spiritual growth and ministry over the years of our separation. For a time he had been imprisoned for his faith. He had spent time in the highlands in tribal villages, learning the people's language, planting churches. Today those churches are experiencing explosive growth.

As Donna and I conversed with Dinh and his wife, hearing their stories of sacrifice, faith and courage, we cried. It seemed just like another chapter in the book of Acts! We saw the glory of Christ reflected from Dinh's face. We entered into the joy of his spiritual victories. And an unforgettable impression gripped our hearts. Investment in the lives of people—people like Dinh—is what missionary work is all about! We could say to Dinh, in Paul's words, "What is . . . the crown in which we will glory in the presence of our Lord Jesus when he comes? Is it not you? Indeed, you are our glory and joy."

This prospect has motivated me to invest more of my time and energy in people. They are the one real prize that will provide us immeasurable joy at the coming of our Lord Jesus Christ. In training national Christians, it is not enough that we equip them to evangelize. We must take them one step further by training them also to evangelize cross-culturally. We must help them catch a vision of cross-cultural missions. We must ignite in them the passion to take the gospel to another people group or another nation. Dr. Ralph D. Winter, who heads the U.S. Center for World Mission in Pasadena, California, once said to me, "The ultimate measure of a missionary's success is that the Christians on his or her mission field become missionaries themselves."

Dinh was such a person. He had caught the vision and passion of missions. He was doing missionary work even in the absence of his North American mentor.

I need to make it clear that I was not the only Western missionary in Vietnam investing in such eternal crowns. A number of Vietnamese Christians had been trained to serve cross-culturally. Some were working among the Montagnards—the tribal peoples in the highlands of South Vietnam. Others had gone as missionaries to neighboring Laos and even to France.

Let me ask you: When you meet Christ at heaven's gate, will there be also those whom you had a part in preparing for heaven? Or will you arrive alone?

Whether you are winning neighbors across the street or neighbors across the sea, remember one thing. They are people. You are winning *people* to Christ. To do this you need to give attention to *positioning* yourself to reach people. You must *penetrate* their lives culturally. You must patiently *prepare* yourself for effective communication. Finally, you must unswervingly commit yourself to focus your time and energies on eternal *prizes*—people!

What kind of a prize will you rejoice in on that glorious crowning day? Will there be anyone who will come up to you to thank you for your part in winning him or her to faith in Jesus Christ?

Are you a missionary who wins?

Study Guide Questions

1. In what four ways might a missionary emulate Paul as a "bond servant"? Why is this important for the missionary who wants to become an effective communicator of the gospel?

2. How might these same principles apply to the sending church?

3. Why is a missionary's first term often the most difficult? What might his or her sending church do to help ease the difficulties?

4. What did identification or acculturation mean for the apostle Paul? How does it apply to today's missionary? Can the same concept apply to an effective witness here at home? How?

5. What preparatory steps are essential if today's missionary is to be effective?

6. How do children learn to speak their mother tongue? How might that method be applied to the missionary's language study?

7. What is your reaction to this statement: "As a shepherd feeds his sheep and those sheep give birth to lambs, so the missionary trains national Christians and the national Christians evangelize their own people"?

8. What do you think is the "prize," the "crown that will last forever" (1 Corinthians 9:24-25) that Paul sought to win? How might this thought motivate people in our homeland churches?

Chapter Six

Work That Is Worth Doing

First Corinthians 1-15

N EXT TO A PERSON'S NAME, PROBABLY nothing sets an individual apart like his or her work. When we meet someone for the first time, one of our first questions likely will be, "And what do you do?" Meaning, "What is your work, your major occupation?"

In a Labor Day address, former President Teddy Roosevelt remarked, "Far and away the best prize that life offers is a chance to work hard at work *worth doing.*" But what kind of work is work worth doing?

While I was still very young, my father taught me the value of work. I will forever be grateful for his lessons. He told me God's Word teaches that any person who won't work shouldn't eat. So, as a member of the family, I was expected to do certain tasks: keep my room clean, help with the dishes, put the garbage out, mow the lawn, shovel the snow, wash the car.

I was the youngest of Dad and Mom's seven children. Dad assured me that as long as my feet were under his table, he would provide me with everything I *needed*. He made clear the distinction between needs and wants. For the wants, he suggested I could find jobs outside the home such as delivering newspapers, mowing lawns, shoveling snow or caddying at the golf course. Like any healthy, active boy, I developed numerous wants. I wanted a top-quality first-baseman's mitt, so I earned the money for it. Of course, I took better care of my glove than some of my friends did theirs. The reason? I had worked hard to buy it.

I decided I wanted a new suit. In Dad's estimation, a new suit was not a necessity. If I wanted one, I could earn the money and buy a suit, which I did. I also earned money to buy some fancy sports shirts and sweaters that fell within the same category. I took especially good care of each item.

As my junior year of high school approached, my parents were preparing to return to Vietnam. As I mentioned earlier, they gave me the choice of completing high school at Dalat, Vietnam, or at Hampden DuBose Academy, Zellwood, Florida. Dalat was a school founded for missionaries' children; Dad and Mother's sponsoring mission would cover the costs. At Hampden DuBose Academy, I would need a work scholarship. By then I was accustomed to work. I decided on Hampden DuBose. For two years I worked very hard mowing lawns, waiting on tables, washing dishes, sawing and splitting logs, maintaining and driving the school's cars and pickup. During those two years I learned to actually enjoy hard work.

When I graduated, I wanted to go on to college to train for Christian ministry. There was no way my parents, on their missionary income, could put me through college. Dad had worked his way through; why couldn't I? My first summer I lived with a friend who had graduated the year before. He drove a bakery truck and I, a coal truck. No work could have been dirtier or much harder than driving that coal truck. But through that job God was providing college tuition, and I learned to love the work.

Arriving at Nyack College, I found a job working three nights a week at a local box factory. It was dirty, tiring, monotonous work lasting until 1:30 a.m., but it paid the continuing school bills. The next three years I did other jobs. I traveled for a summer with the Ambassadors Quartet, representing the college. I wrapped packages in a gift mail-order business. I drove a delivery truck for a grocery store. I janitored for a pharmaceutical laboratory. For every job I praised God and worked conscientiously. As far as I was concerned, I was working for God first and for my employer second.

One of my college summers I drove a truck and sold Dr. Pepper and Suncrest beverages in Burlington, Iowa. My employer offered a watch to the salesperson who would sell the most. The territory was full of empty bottles left when the previous owner went bankrupt. One of the salesmen, who badly wanted to win the watch, came up with an idea: He told his customers he would pick up *two* cases of empty bottles for every case of pop they bought. I, too, was interested in the watch. I asked God to help me devise a better plan—one that would at the same time please my customers. I offered no deals. Instead, I gave each customer a free cold sample of our beverage while I picked up *all* their empties—no limit. After I had the bottles loaded on the truck, I asked them how they enjoyed the drink. Then I told them they had a credit of "X" dollars in bottles. My efforts to put my customers' interests first and to treat them with kindness paid off. Almost to a person, they bought that amount of beverage from me. At the end of summer, I got the watch, and my employer asked me to stay on as sales supervisor. I thanked him sincerely. I also thanked the Lord for valuable lessons learned and for providing my tuition for another semester of college.

The summer after my third year of college, Donna and I were married. She had graduated; I had two years to go, including a year of postgraduate studies. Leland R. Harper, the college's business manager, asked me if I would manage the campus store, called The Hub. His invitation came as a great surprise. I had had neither business training nor experience, but Mr. Harper offered to advise me. Since I was carrying a heavy academic load, Donna worked 40 hours a week behind the counter, and I worked 20 hours supervising our employees, purchasing food items and stocking shelves. Once again, I asked God for wisdom. I prayed that the store would turn a profit that would please and glorify Him.

Two years later I graduated. In five years I had completed the requirements for two degrees: bachelor of science and bachelor of theology. I also graduated with a wife, a baby, a furnished apartment and a relatively new car—all debt-free. I thanked Mr. Harper for the work he had provided me at The Hub. He said the two years Donna and I had managed the store were the first years The Hub had come out in the black! God had answered prayer with wisdom and blessing.

Work. Missionary work. Even before graduation, The Christian and Missionary Alliance had come to Donna and me with an unusual request. Would we be willing to leave at once for Vietnam without the two years of home service usually required? Suddenly our missionary careers, once comfortably off in the future, were almost upon us!

I began to think more seriously about missions. What exactly was missionary work like? I had spent my first eight years observing my missionary father at work, but childhood impressions can be deceiving. During my senior year of college I had spent hours in First Corinthians, reading, digging, meditating. For reasons unknown to me at the time, the term *work* and the passages dealing with the work theme seemed to jump out at me. It was as though the Lord was preparing me for what lay ahead of me as a missionary, evangelist and pastor. Today, as I review those Bible texts and look back across 40 years of ministry, I can see that God's Word then became the guiding principles in the missionary work Donna and I have been privileged to do.

The thesis of this chapter is simple. If we will cooperate with Him, *God has a valuable, fulfilling and lasting work that He wants to accomplish* in *and* through *us.* Paul seems to be describing that work with four adjectives: internal, eternal, spiritual and bountiful. We'll use those four adjectives as we examine the missionary's work.

1. Internal Work

What, after all, is Apollos? And what is Paul? Only servants, through whom you came to believe—as the Lord has assigned to each his task. I planted the seed, Apollos watered it, but God made it grow. So neither he who plants nor he who waters is anything, but only God, who makes things grow. The man who plants and the man who waters have one purpose, and each will be rewarded according to his own labor. For we are God's fellow workers; you are God's field, God's building. (3:5-9)

Missionary Work Is First and Foremost God's Work

Planting and watering are external operations. Giving life and bringing growth are internal. Paul and Apollos were workers with God, but theirs was the visible, external work. On the other hand, God's work—giving life and bringing growth—though invisible, was what really counted and thus was foremost.

From the context we are aware that Paul was dealing with divisiveness that had crept into the Corinthian church. It arose because members placed too much emphasis on the human ministers. Some Corinthian believers claimed to be followers of Paul. Others followed Apollos. Still others, Peter. Paul reminded them that these human ministers were but servants of God who planted and watered. God was the One really responsible for their spiritual life and growth. He alone must receive their glory and praise.

Missionaries are highly honored to be called "fellow workers with God." And if you are a missionary, God may indeed be pleased to work through you. But it is absolutely crucial that you understand that anything lasting is God's work. Paul says the ones who plant and water are really nothing. It is God who gives life and brings about growth.

When Donna and I moved to Tuy Hoa, I purchased a large map of Phu Yen Province and mounted it prominently in my office. I began to plan how I would systematically evangelize village after village. At towns where I knew there were Christians, I pinned flags. Then I marked the villages near each of those flags where I intended to work. I prayed daily for those towns and villages. But I really was asking God to bless *my* work, not show me where He wanted to accomplish *His* work.

I began to preach in those villages I had flagged. But nothing happened. No one believed.

Then one day a Christian came from one of the villages I had flagged. Would Pastor Nguyen van Thin and I go to a village where some of his relatives lived? They were asking questions about the gospel. It was a village I had not marked. But obviously God was working in the hearts of some of the people there. In a month's time, God had brought to repentance and faith some 100 people! From then on, I tried to be more sensitive as to where God wanted me to work. I found this new approach much more glorifying to God. After all, it was first and foremost His work, not mine or Pastor Thin's.

Missionary work is primarily internal. God is more concerned with what He is doing *in* us than what we may want Him to do *through* us. The Corinthians were enamored by the externals of what Paul and Apollos had accomplished in their midst. But Paul pointed them to the internals of what God had done within them. He reminded the Corinthians that they were a field in which God was at work. They were a building God was constructing.

I confess that when I arrived in Tuy Hoa to launch "my missionary career," I was quite taken by that map on my office wall. I was sure God would accomplish much through me in Phu Yen Province. For some reason, God was more concerned about His work of grace in Donna's heart and mine. As the Master Farmer, He set about to work the unproductive soil of our lives. He wanted to produce a harvest of righteousness for His glory and purposes. We would not have chosen the tools He used. Often they were painful and sometimes frustrating.

Likewise the processes God used were painful. We were tested physically. Flash floods took our treasures. Heightened Vietcong activity played on our emotions. A moral failure involving our cook and our language teacher was a keen disappointment. Months of low income and high expenses stressed us financially.

I realized later that God was using these trials to make us more like His Son, Jesus Christ.

"In all things God works for the good of those who love him, who have been called according to his purpose" (Romans 8:28). Did you catch those two words, *God works*? Part of the purpose of God's work is that we might be "conformed to the likeness of his Son" (8:29).

God was doing in Donna and me exactly what Paul, centuries earlier, said He was doing in the Philippian Christians: "He who began a good work in you will carry it on to completion until the day of Christ Jesus" (Philippians 1:6). "It is God who works in you to will and to act according to his good purpose" (2:13).

On one furlough from Vietnam, I traveled with Floyd Bowman, a missionary to West Africa, as we visited a number of North American churches. He had worked in Timbuktu, Mali, for 10 years before he saw a single convert. As he told his story, it was clear to me that God was working all 10 of those years. He was working *in* Floyd Bowman so that He could work *through* him in more marvelous and mighty ways. Traveling with that godly missionary, I saw undeniable evidence of God's handiwork.

2. Eternal Work

Pat Kelly, who later became a gospel evangelist, played major league baseball with the Baltimore Orioles. His manager was the fiery, successful Earl Weaver. Weaver, like many top sports skippers, kept his mind on one thing: winning.

One day Kelly stopped to talk with his manager.

"Weave," Kelly said, "it sure is good to walk with Jesus."

"That's nice," the manager replied, "but I'd rather you would walk with the bases loaded."

Could two men's perspectives be more different? If we see life as temporal, we can become preoccupied with the things of this earth. We forget that this life is but preparation for eternity. If we have the eternal view, we will be working for God's purposes and glory.[1]

Notice in First Corinthians 3 how Paul contrasts two kinds of work: work that is temporal, perishing and relatively worthless, and work that is eternal and priceless:

By the grace God has given me, I laid a foundation as an expert builder, and someone else is building on it. But each one should be careful how he builds. For no one can lay any foundation other than the one already laid, which is Jesus Christ. If any man builds on this foundation using gold, silver, costly stones, wood, hay or straw, his work will be shown for what it is, because the Day will bring it to light. It will be revealed with fire, and the fire will test the quality of each man's work. If what he has built survives, he will receive his reward. If it is burned up, he will suffer loss; he himself will be saved, but only as one escaping through the flames. (3:10-15)

Much Missionary Work Is Temporal

Paul, like any missionary today, did some tasks that were temporal in nature. They were necessary for this life, but in relation to the next life they were of no value. "We work hard with our own hands," he told the Corinthians (4:12). Later he asked, "Is it only I and Barnabas who must work for a living?" (9:6). We know that the work to which he refers was tentmaking (Acts 18:3). This he did to support himself—to put bread on the table.

So today, much that a missionary does is simply to sustain physical life. While such work is necessary, the missionary must be careful that it doesn't consume all of his or her time and energy. Some of the most frustrating times in a missionary's life are those days when it seems all he or she accomplishes falls under the category of making tents. The Jeep needs overhauling. The leaking roof must be repaired. Letters have to be written. Bills must be paid (yes, even overseas!). Literature must be printed. And the list goes on.

Some Missionary Work Must Be Eternal

In chapter 3 Paul wrote about the silver, gold and precious stones that survive the testing fire and for which there would be rewards. In chapter 9, he told the Corinthian believers *they* were his work. He then went on to describe his burning passion to win people to Christ because people were the real, imperishable crown for which he labored.

People are really what missionary work is all about. People must be won to Christ. People must be discipled. People must be integrated into the church. People must be sent out to reach and win and disciple other people. So the missionary must constantly keep checking to determine how much of his or her efforts are invested in people. People are the only truly eternal work.

Let me emphasize what I just said. *People are the missionary's real work.* Tentmaking is what the missionary may have to do to keep body and soul together. When time is no more and we are suddenly face to face with God in eternity, all the tents will have gone up in smoke. Only the people we have impacted for God will be left.

I had a little preview of that awesome Day when South Vietnam fell to the communists. Suddenly I was cut off from my missionary work of 20 years. I stood on the deck of the aircraft carrier *Vancouver* and looked back at the coast of Vietnam where I had served. I realized then that what really mattered were the people I had led to Christ. What really mattered were the young men I had discipled at the youth center in Hue. What really mattered were the families in Phu Yen Province who had been transformed by the gospel. What really mattered were the villages in

An-Loc Province that had turned from idols to serve the living God. Those redeemed people were the "gold, silver, costly stones" calculated to survive the testing fires.

Is your work all tentmaking? Or are there people whom you are impacting for God and eternity? When you pass into the next life you will leave behind the house you live in, the clubs you belong to, your checkbook, your financial investments. None of those things will follow you into the next life. In what kind of activities are you involved? Do they have about them anything eternal?

Are you considering missionary work? What will be the focus of your life work? Are you already a career missionary? What *is* your emphasis? I exhort you, from Paul's words to the Corinthians, to invest your life in people. If you will make that kind of an investment, your work will last forever. It will gladden your heart and bring glory to God!

3. Spiritual Work

True worshipers must worship God in spirit. True witnesses must witness in the power of God's Spirit. So those who serve God must work under the gifting of the Holy Spirit. With the coming of the Spirit at Pentecost, spiritual service shifted to where it really belonged. Before, it was the keeping of holy days, the wearing of prescribed garments, the observance of ceremony. Suddenly it was the union of the human spirit and the Spirit of God! And with that union, God gave gifts to the church. In Paul's counsel to the Corinthians concerning spiritual gifts we find the next important references to work and working. Notice the words "service," "working," "works," "the work":

> Now about spiritual gifts, brothers, I do not want you to be ignorant. You know that when you were pagans, somehow or other you were influenced and led astray to mute idols. Therefore I tell you that no one who is speaking by the Spirit of God says, "Jesus be cursed," and no one can say, "Jesus is Lord," except by the Holy Spirit.
> There are different kinds of gifts, but the same Spirit. There are different kinds of service, but the same Lord. There are different kinds of working, but the same God works all of them in all men. . . .
> All these are the work of one and the same Spirit. (12:1-6, 11)

Two things are crystal clear in the above Scripture: (1) If work is to be eternal, it must be done in the Spirit. (2) If our work is to be done in the Spirit, Christ must be Lord of our lives.

Missionaries Must Minister in Their Area of Giftedness.

God is pleased to grant to every member of

Christ's body spiritual gifts that will enable that member to do His work in His way for His desired results! Spiritual gifts are divinely given abilities to be used within the body to build up Christ's body. They are to be used outside the body to reach lost people for Christ.

It is a marvelous experience to see God at work through gifted missionaries. There is a delight and a buoyancy in their work that can't be interpreted in human terms. On the other hand, when they are ministering outside of their gifts, there is a strain and a drag that is not of the Spirit.

My sister, Anne Moore, is unusually gifted in art and music. From her earliest years her gifts were apparent. When she and her husband, David, served as missionaries in Indonesia, they were appointed to teach in one of the Bible schools. Teaching is one of David's gifts. He felt fulfilled. God wonderfully used him as a teacher. But Anne grew more frustrated with every passing day. At last she petitioned the field executive committee to release her from teaching responsibilities and allow her to use her gifts of art and music. The committee agreed to her request, and Anne began composing Christian lyrics set to Indonesian-style music. Church people loved these new choruses. They were published in a chorus book that had wide circulation throughout Indonesia. And Anne? Excitement and joy replaced her earlier frustration.

Some years later, David joined the faculty of Jaffray School of Missions (now Alliance Theological Seminary). Soon Anne became art editor for her denomination's magazine, *Alliance Life.* Again her gifts were very much appreciated.

I consider evangelism to be my special gift. I mentioned in an earlier chapter that a Vietnamese pastor was first to recognize my gift. Missionary colleagues came to agree with him. Increasingly, as God made my ministry fruitful, I was invited to hold evangelistic crusades throughout South Vietnam.

Many times I preached, witnessed and taught all day, sometimes late into the night as well. People would ask me where I found strength for such a grueling schedule. I have but one reply: When I serve in the area of my giftedness, God gives unusual delight and energy. When I expend the same amount of time and energy in work outside my giftedness, I become exhausted and burned out.

Missionaries Must Submit to Christ's Lordship

Much is being written today about discovering and using one's gift in ministry. I have no objection. Counsel like that is needed. But equal emphasis must be placed on allowing Christ His rightful place in our lives as Lord. Paul said, "No one can say, 'Jesus is Lord,' except by the Holy Spirit." This needs to be a daily commitment.

On the Day of Pentecost, Peter explained the Spirit's filling of the believers in these words:

> God has raised this Jesus to life, and we are all witnesses of the fact. Exalted to the right hand of God, he has received from the Father the promised Holy Spirit and has poured out what you now see and hear (Acts 2:32-33).

We want God's Spirit to fill us and use us for His purposes and glory. What Peter described as happening corporately to the 120 people in the upper room on the Day of Pentecost, Paul says must happen to each of us individually. That is, we must surrender to Christ and exalt Him as Lord of our lives. If He is not in control of us, we cannot expect Him to express His gifts in us to their fullest.

The time came when I understood and experienced what it means to enthrone Christ as Lord. I have sought to renew that commitment daily. Occasionally I have allowed other things unconsciously to creep into my life. (I need to be honest and call them *sins*.) I say "unconsciously," because some of the things—sins—that crept in were not easy to recognize. I'm speaking of half-truths, unkind attitudes, unfounded fears of people, impure second glances, subtle pride. But, praise God, in His faithfulness He by His Spirit brings necessary conviction. Then it is up to us to respond.

Both from the Word and from personal experience, I cannot emphasize enough the importance of Christ's constant lordship. The Spirit gives gifts to the church, yes! But it is my deep conviction that those gifts can only be experienced fully by the person wholly yielded to God's control. Then and only then can we offer to Him truly spiritual work, truly . . .

4. Bountiful Work

As I continued my search of First Corinthians, I came to another reference to the word *work*. It is at the end of the great resurrection chapter.

> Therefore, my dear brothers, stand firm. Let nothing move you. Always give yourselves fully to the work of the Lord, because you know that your labor in the Lord is not in vain. (15:58)

The revered King James version translates "Always give yourselves fully to the work of the Lord," ". . . always abounding in the work of the Lord." Faith in the resurrection of Jesus from the dead, Paul says, ought to lead to bountiful, fruitful work. There is nothing narrow or cramped about the Christian's life and work. It is to be both abundant and abounding. In 15:58 two facets of abounding work stand out: (1) It is to be work done in perspective. (2) It is to be persevering work.

Missionary Work Must Be Done in Perspective

What is the perspective that Paul suggests for our work? Notice the context of the verse. It follows Paul's tremendous message about Christ's triumphant resurrection and the believer's future victory. Because Jesus lives, we, too, shall rise from the dead to live forever. And because God will ultimately triumph, our *work* is not in vain.

Much missionary work, not unlike other Christian ministry, is done in relative obscurity. Only God sees it. That is good, because it is the way God would have it. Often missionary work doesn't seem to bear fruit. That can be frustrating unless the missionary keeps his work in proper perspective. Christ is coming again! We who are alive and remain shall rise to meet Him in the air! We will hear His "Well done!" Our labor in the Lord is not in vain!

Occasionally I have been involved in missionary work that seemed in vain. There were no apparent results. Later—sometimes many years later—I discovered how wrong I had been. Learning of positive results many years afterward has encouraged me. Probably some of the other tasks I regarded as fruitless were not.

Once I was preaching at a place called Cho-Gia, where we had a small nucleus of believers. In our house-to-house witness I ran into a Chinese pharmacist who with great enthusiasm prayed to receive Christ. About an hour later the man came looking for me.

"I'm sorry," he apologized, "but I must give up my new faith. When my wife learned what I did, she took a knife and threatened to kill me. There's no way I can continue." Nothing I said would change his mind.

Then, about 10 years later, I had opportunity to preach again in that area. Who should be the first to greet me but my Chinese pharmacist! He had a Bible and a hymnbook under his arm and a smile almost as bright as the sun.

"Do you remember me?" he asked.

"You aren't the pharmacist at Cho-Gia, are you?" I queried.

"So you *do* remember!" he exclaimed. He went on to tell me that sometime after we had moved from the area, his wife had become a believer. "In fact," he added, "our whole family has become Christians!"

You can imagine my surprise and joy. The evangelistic visit in his home had not been in vain after all!

Missionary Work Must Be Persevering

William Carey, whose pioneer labors in India are legendary, was asked how he managed to accomplish so much.

"I can plod," the celebrated missionary replied. Perseverance is a quality high on the list of every successful missionary.

I am not surprised, therefore, that the greatest human missionary of all time should write to the Corinthians: "Let nothing move you. Always give yourselves fully to the work of the Lord." The Corinthian believers were prone to be fickle. They shifted allegiance from one leader to another, from one task to another. They needed to focus on Christ's resurrection and God's desire to save humankind, Paul was saying. Then they would not be so easily shaken.

No two people better exemplify this quality of perseverance than my late parents, missionaries to Vietnam before me. Dad had little formal education, but he became an avid reader. He inherited his father-in-law's large library and devoured book after book: history, biography, theology, sermons by great preachers. He subscribed to a number of periodicals to keep abreast of the times.

Dad was also a man of the Book, studying the Word daily. Each year he read consecutively the entire Bible. And Dad was a man of prayer. In addition to family worship each evening, he spent much time in private prayer.

Mom likewise exhibited unusual perseverance. Bearing seven children within 12 years didn't deter her from participating with Dad in missionary service. And until we were old enough for boarding school, she took us children along on their preaching missions.

When Mom developed a heart condition several years after my birth, doctors tried to slow her down. But nothing could keep her from her family and missionary duties. She was 61 when she and Dad returned to the States in 1954. The examining doctor couldn't believe how many things were wrong with Mom! She and Dad gave themselves to fervent, persevering prayer. A year later, the same doctor cleared her to go back to Vietnam!

In 1960 Dad and Mom "retired" from missionary service. So what did they do? They planted a church in Maryland. On Christmas Eve, 1964, when the church was well established and her work was completed, Mom fell asleep in the strong arms of Jesus.

Dad and Mom's bountiful work for God, their eternal perspective and astounding persistence has had an undeniable impact upon my life and ministry. They "stood firm" in their missionary calling. They "let nothing move them" from completing the task committed to them. They "always gave of themselves fully to the work of the Lord."

Perhaps that is one reason why six of their seven children heard God's call and followed in their missionary footsteps. Perhaps it is one reason why each of those children discovered and became involved in work worth doing.

Study Guide Questions

1. What does Paul mean by his statement that he and Apollos were "God's fellow work-

ers?" How does it apply to today's missionary?

2. What is the difference between God's blessing *our* work and God's accomplishing *His* work through us? How does this relate to God's glory?

3. What are some of the temporal tasks today's missionary must do? What, in contrast, is the eternal work that he or she must ever keep in focus?

4. Define your understanding of "the gifts of the Spirit" as the expression was used in this book chapter. How significant to missionary work today are these spiritual gifts? Explain.

5. How might the lordship of Christ in a missionary's life impact the effectiveness of his or her work? How might the lordship of Christ apply to you and your work?

6. How do you see the principle of perspective applying to a missionary's work? to your work?

7. What is one of the least appreciated yet most essential qualities of an effective missionary? How does that quality relate to your work with and for Christ?

Endnotes

1. *Our Daily Bread* (Grand Rapids, MI: Radio Bible Class Ministries July, 1992).

Chapter Seven

How You Can Be Effective

First Corinthians 16:1-11

IN OUR CHILDHOOD MOST OF US LEARNED a simple prayer that we recited at bedtime:

> Now I lay me down to sleep;
> I pray Thee, Lord, my soul to keep.
> And if I die before I wake,
> I pray Thee, Lord, my soul to take.

Thomas Osborne Davis has written a sequel that one might recite before starting a new work day:

> Now I get me up to work;
> I pray Thee, Lord, I may not shirk.
> And if I die before tonight,
> I pray my work will be all right.

In our last chapter we focused on the *What*

of missionary work. In this chapter, we shall zero in on the *How*. How can a missionary work so effectively that God will say it's "all right"?

There is a significant difference between being efficient and being effective. The efficient missionary does things right; the effective missionary does right things. Ideally, the effective missionary does things right *and* does right things. He or she does the right work in the right way. But we are human. Keeping such a balance is not easy. Given a choice, the missionary will do well to focus his or her energies on being effective.

In the sport of archery, efficiency is a well-polished bow and arrow and a perfectly painted target. Effectiveness is hitting the target. In fact, it is hitting the bull's-eye. It is possible to spend all one's time tightening the bow, polishing the arrows, adjusting the target without ever hitting the bull's-eye. For a missionary, it is possible to do everything efficiently without ever really "hitting the target"—that is, accomplishing what Christ sent him or her to do.

Some critics might say John the Baptist didn't do too many things right. He wore odd clothes; he ate strange food; he lived and preached in out-of-the-way places. He made some rather cutting remarks. But he prepared the way for Jesus. He pointed others to Jesus as the Lamb of God who takes away the sin of the world.

I knew a missionary who spoke the local language so poorly that national pastors had to repeat his sermons in capsule form in order for the congregation to understand what he had said. I saw him make some serious cultural mistakes. Yet the man had a very fruitful ministry. He loved Jesus and he loved the people. He didn't do some things right, but he did the right things. He was not very efficient, but he was very effective!

In chapter 6 we described missionary work with four adjectives: *internal, eternal, spiritual* and *abounding.* In this chapter I want to suggest a fifth adjective for missionary work: *effective.* We found the first four adjectives in chapters 3, 12 and 15 of First Corinthians. We find the adjective *effective* in chapter 16. Paul says, "A great door for effective work has opened to me" (16:9).

God desires to do effective work through His missionaries. That, in short, is the thesis of this chapter. As I studied First Corinthians 16, I discovered five facets of effective work. These usually set apart the missionary whose work is truly effective. They mark the missionary who lives and works "by the Book." I will use five words to sum up those five facets of effective work: *offerings, opposition, openness, occupancy* and *others.* Let's take them in that order.

1. Offerings

Paul begins, "Now about the collection for God's people: Do what I told the Galatian churches to do" (16:1). God's servant should never be afraid to ask God's people to share financially in God's work. To do eternal work effectively demands temporal resources. Not everyone can travel across an ocean or minister cross-culturally, but all can share in missionary work.

The process operates this way: Christian farmers, carpenters, factory workers, secretaries, business people, professionals work at their tasks and receive appropriate financial returns for that work. Realizing that they are stewards—managers—of those financial resources God has entrusted to them, they invest some of their income in world missions. Those dollars go in part to the support of missionaries and their work. In this way the Christians' work is translated into missionary work through the marvelous medium of currency. Thus we have an interdependency between Christians in the homeland and the missionary in a foreign land. Christians at home rely on the missionary to be their witness to people who have not heard of Christ. The missionary relies on the Christians at home to supply the money that will keep him or her working overseas.

My missionary father was never reluctant to ask God's people to share financially in his work. When I questioned Dad about the propriety of such appeals, he responded, "I'm not asking for myself. I'm asking for God's work. God's people want to be involved in that work.

But how can they invest if I don't tell them of the opportunities?" And Dad was right!

In 1955, as Dad and Mom were returning to Vietnam for their last term of service, they needed a vehicle for their work. Dad didn't have any funds for a car, so in one of his circular letters sent to interested friends, he wrote: "If any of you should have a 1953 or 1954 Ford that you would like to invest in our missionary work, please let me know. I'll come pick it up and ship it to Vietnam for our ministry there."

A retired Christian, then up in years, received Dad's letter. He had been looking for something he could do for missions. He was driving a 1953 Ford.

"I have the car you're looking for," he wrote to Dad. That 1953 Ford served Dad and Mom magnificently until they retired from Vietnam in 1960.

During that final term another critical need arose. Dad had been either renting or building "preaching chapels" where he could hold evangelistic meetings and plant new churches. But his funds for this purpose were exhausted. He went to bed discouraged and during the night had a dream. In his dream he saw a large tent filled with people listening to the gospel. Many responded to the message, receiving Christ into their lives. Until then tent meetings had never entered Dad's mind. But he at once composed another circular letter to his friends back home: "If any of you should have a large tent that you could send to Vietnam for evangelistic meetings, I would be most grateful. I would use it to plant churches up and down the coast of Vietnam."

What individual would have a tent large enough for Dad's purpose? On Dad's mailing list was a Mr. Adams. Dad had never met him, but another missionary had asked Dad to add Adams' name to his mailing list. Mr. Adams was the leader of an evangelistic team called Fishers of Men. At age 70, he was about to retire. But what would he do with his almost-new tent? While he was praying for God's direction, Dad's letter arrived.

Donna and I had the privilege of taking that tent to Vietnam as a part of our baggage. We helped Dad set it up for the first crusade in Hue, the city where I had been born. When Dad retired, he turned the tent over to me for use in my evangelistic ministry.

No, God's servants overseas should never be reticent to ask God's people at home to share in the support of God's work. Their gifts usually will make the missionary's work much more effective.

Nor should homeland Christians be reticent to invest generously in God's work abroad. In 16:2-4, Paul enumerates two vital principles regarding such investments. One is *the principle of generosity*. The other is *the principle of accountability*.

The Principle of Generosity

Paul writes: "On the first day of every week,

each one of you should set aside a sum of money in keeping with his income, saving it up, so that when I come no collections will have to be made" (16:2).

In a subsequent letter, Paul would tell the Corinthians about the generous assistance Macedonian believers gave to famine-stricken Christians in Judea: "Out of the most severe trial, their overflowing joy and their extreme poverty welled up in rich generosity" (2 Corinthians 8:2). He goes on to say of them, "They gave as much as they were able, and even beyond their ability. Entirely on their own, they urgently pleaded with us for the privilege of sharing in this service to the saints" (2 Corinthians 8:3-4).

Today the churches of South Korea are a model of generous, sacrificial giving. For years South Korea was ravished by war. Yet some of the largest, most dynamic churches in the world are in South Korea. Part of the reason is their commitment to sacrificial, generous giving. Some while back, *Our Daily Bread* related the story of one such Korean congregation. The church had grown as much as possible without enlarging its building. In a special service set apart for that purpose, people brought their building fund gifts to the front of the church. One older woman went forward with her rice bowl and chopsticks.

"Mama, you can't give those," the pastor remonstrated. "They are all you possess."

But the little woman insisted. "You take them," she said.

As the pastor stood before the congregation, holding the rice bowl and the two chopsticks, one of her Christian brothers stood up and announced, "I'll give you 6,500,000 won [approximately $10,000]."[1]

The Principle of Accountability

Generous giving will lead to effective work only if it is done with responsibility and accountability. For that reason, Paul gave clear instructions to the Corinthian church to make sure their money was contributed and used for its intended purpose:

> Then, when I arrive, I will give letters of introduction to the men you approve and send them with your gift to Jerusalem. If it seems advisable for me to go also, they will accompany me. (16:3-4)

In 25 years of missionary service I saw much generous giving. I also saw both responsible and irresponsible handling of money. The mission with which I served— The Christian and Missionary Alliance—exercised extreme care to guarantee accountability and wise investment of every missionary dollar. I am not the least hesitant to invest my missionary giving through The Christian and Missionary Alliance.

Alas! Not all organizations practice such careful accountability. While I was ministering in Hong Kong, an "independent" missionary, who loved boats, raised money to buy a large, double-decked ferryboat that had been used to transport cars across Hong Kong harbor. His alleged purpose for the acquisition was to evangelize Hong Kong's youth by offering them harbor cruises. Indeed, the boat was used for that purpose—not very often, but it happened. I personally spoke a few times to the groups until I realized the missionary was doing very little to follow up the new believers or integrate them into any of the local churches. He was accountable to no one but himself. The lack of accountability led to ineffective missionary work and irresponsible use of money. No doubt much of the money that went into his boat had been sacrificially given.

I hope you are giving both generously and sacrificially to extend Christ's kingdom in other lands. I also hope you have checked to make sure your missionary giving is being invested responsibly for effective work overseas.

2. Opposition

The next aspect of effective work that sets apart a missionary living and working "by the Book" is opposition. Whenever God is at work, Satan is working overtime to stop, or at least to hinder, Him. Paul experienced it:

I will stay on at Ephesus until Pentecost, because a great door for effective work has opened to me, and there are many who oppose me. (16:8-9)

Acts 19 covers this same time period. Amid a very fruitful ministry Paul was maligned by obstinate listeners who set the whole city in an uproar. In fact, Paul was confronted by opposition wherever he attempted to work. We discover a similar pattern throughout church history.

Today missionary work is no different. As a missionary in Vietnam and later in Hong Kong, I could almost predict when God was about to do something unusual. All I had to do was observe the degree of difficulty we were encountering.

One of the most fruitful evangelistic crusades I was ever involved in took place in the provincial capital of Quang Ngai on the central coast of Vietnam. It was after Dad had retired, and I was using the tent he passed on to me. To help promote the crusade, a Christian GI offered to print tens of thousands of leaflets and to drop them by plane all over the city. Just as he released the leaflets, a severe gust of wind blew the papers out into the communist-infested countryside far from our intended target. We erected the tent in a park across the street from the provincial headquarters. Never had we found such a strategic location for our meetings. But a sudden typhoon dumped six inches of flood water into the tent and nearly blew the tent away. For a moment we thought we should cancel the crusade. Instead, we prayed that God would somehow work in spite of the difficulties.

After three days the rain stopped. The provincial chief attended our opening meeting. Every night the tent was packed solid. Scores of people went forward to receive Christ. But the most amazing part came *after* the meetings ended. Numbers of people from the countryside began coming to the local church, inquiring of the pastor where the services were being held. They had found the wind-blown leaflets and had come to town to hear the good news of Jesus!

The meetings were over. But each person who inquired, the pastor invited into the parsonage for a cup of tea. As he shared the gospel, many of these trusted Christ for salvation. In fact, a number of them became a new church congregation out in the countryside!

Roses are known for their thorns. Pearls develop where the oysters are irritated. Diamonds form under intense pressure. And effective spiritual ministry often takes place amid unusual difficulties. That brings us to the third aspect of effective work:

3. Openness

Openness is the third facet of effective work for God. Paul describes openness in these words:

I will stay on at Ephesus until Pentecost, because a great door for effective work has opened to me. (16:8-9)

Have you noticed? When all is calm and everything is going well, people are resistant to the gospel. But let life be chaotic and fraught with reverses, and people are much more responsive and open.

I'm writing these lines in Berlin, Germany, in the home of a Vietnamese Christian refugee. Nguyen duc Hoa is his name. He is a painter. Let me quote a part of Hoa's personal testimony:

I accepted Christ as my Savior on a still, dark night in which no moon or stars were in the sky. I was in a boat that had run aground on a river sandbar not far from Vung Tau, Vietnam. . . .

Normally in such a situation, the pilot-owner would reverse the engines and back off. In this case he was afraid the noise of the revving motors would attract unwanted attention. So we lay beached on the sandbar, totally exposed. It was 10 o'clock at night.

A little while later we heard the sound of two communist patrol boats. They came closer and closer, lighting up both banks of the river with their floodlights. By then, the boats were scarcely half a mile from us. Our boat's owner lay groaning on the floor of the cabin.

"Hoa," he said to me, "we'll stay here and wait until they arrest us."

In that desperate situation all those on the boat were fearful. Strangely, I was calm. I suddenly wanted to pray to a Higher Power. So I prayed a short prayer to the Lord. It was the first time in my life I had prayed.

Very softly I said the words: "Save me and the others in this boat so we will not be captured." Not long afterward, the two patrol boats turned around and went away.

About 2 o'clock in the morning the tide came in and we floated free of the sandbar. In our flight we were hunted by many state-owned fishing boats, but with the protection of God we were able to elude them. Some 30 hours later we were rescued by a German ship.

Once in Berlin, I wrote letters to my oldest brother, telling him about the Lord. After a while I received a letter from him saying he had received the Lord as his Savior and had been baptized. . . . Then I received another letter and learned that all my nephews and nieces, one after another, were turning to the Lord as Savior. Besides writing to my relatives, I also wrote to a friend, Dinh cong My, about the Lord Jesus. One day I received a letter from him. As I read it, I knew that only a believer could have written such a letter. Before this, I never cried. Now, every time I learn that someone else has turned to Christ, I find tears running down my face.

I have heard similar stories from Cambodian, Laotian and Hmong refugees. In Cambodia, after more than 50 years of missionary work, there were just 734 baptized believers in the whole country. After the excruciating blood-bath that followed Cambodia's fall to the communists, some 30,000 Cambodians came to Christ in the refugee camps. Today (1995) there are 47 Cambodian churches in the United States and the church in Cambodia is doubling every year!

Southeast Asia has some lessons for us. If tranquility prevails and people seem unresponsive, it is time to be patient and persevering. The harvest will come. When turmoil is evident and uncertainty abounds, we can expect unusual gospel opportunities. That is the time to work zealously to gather in the harvest God desires to give us.

We come very naturally now to the fourth facet of effective work. I shall call it . . .

4. Occupancy

As he wrote from his base in Ephesus, Paul wanted the Corinthians to know that he

planned to visit them. He hoped to spend possibly a whole winter in Corinth. But he could
not allow such a visit to take him away from
Ephesus until his work there was finished. For
the time, he had to continue his occupancy of
Ephesus because God very evidently was at
work in the city. He had to "strike while the
iron was hot." As long as the Ephesians continued to evidence responsiveness, he must continue his work among them. He declared, "I
will stay on at Ephesus until Pentecost, because
a great door for effective work has opened to
me" (16:8-9).

Someone has said that the most important
lesson we learn from history is that we don't
learn from history. We repeat the same mistakes that generations before us have made.

In the late 1940s and early 1950s, when China
was crumbling before the communist on-
slaught, masses of Chinese fled to Taiwan. It
was a time of tremendous difficulty but also
unprecedented opportunity. Like the apostle
Paul, some mission leaders saw the chaos as a
strategic hour for harvest. They knew people
would be unusually responsive—but only for a
limited time. They moved their missionary
forces with the fleeing people in order to reap
that harvest.

Unfortunately, other mission leaders, rather
than moving their missionaries to where the
real action was, redeployed them to other
lands—Thailand, Vietnam, the Philippines, Ja-

pan, Laos. To be sure there were sizable Chinese populations in these other countries, but they were settled and relatively unresponsive.

When I visited Taiwan, I saw firsthand the results. The large Christian churches in Taiwan are associated with the missions who saw the hour of difficulty as an opportunity to be seized, and acted accordingly.

I wish I could say that when Vietnam encountered its similar hour of difficulty and opportunity, we missionaries were moved to where the responsive people were. To a very limited degree and for a much too brief period of time, some of us were assigned to refugee camps on Guam and in the United States. But most of those who remained in missionary service were redeployed to other countries to begin all over again.

It is true that many Vietnamese pastors were among the refugees who fled Vietnam at the time of the communist takeover. That was indeed providential. But they had all they could do learning English, finding jobs, locating housing, placing their children in public schools. They were extremely limited in what they could do to harvest the tremendous number of responsive people.

The world has not seen its last "Vietnam." Political upheavals continue to produce massive groups of refugees in Asia, Eastern Europe and particularly Africa. Along with the privation, emotional anguish and physical suffering are unprecedented opportunities for evangelism. May those responsible for the direction of missionaries not allow history to repeat itself—again. May they keep their "troops" with the responsive peoples and fully enter the wide open doors for effective work.

Of course, if we are to effectively enter these wide open doors and effectively minister in the responsive fields before us, we are going to need the cooperative efforts of . . .

5. Others

Increased opportunity always demands an increased number of effective workers. Paul found it true.

> If Timothy comes, see to it that he has nothing to fear while he is with you, for he is carrying on the work of the Lord, just as I am. No one, then, should refuse to accept him. Send him on his way in peace so that he may return to me. I am expecting him along with the brothers. (16:10-11)

Notice that when Paul encountered a wide-open door of opportunity, he looked for Timothy and other workers to come to his aid. Paul personally had trained Timothy. Now in the hour of need he looked to Timothy to serve with him as a fellow worker. The effective missionary is always enlisting and training workers to help him buy up every opportunity. I see in these verses three vital issues: *cooperation, continuity* and *confidence.*

Cooperation

Paul needed others to help him in his ministry. So he looked for Timothy "along with the brothers" to come to Ephesus and help him reap the harvest he found there. Paul had early discovered the importance of interdependence and cooperation in the body of Christ. It was a guiding principle in all of his work.

Continuity

Paul also saw the need to "pass the baton" to others—to turn over responsibility to younger, capable workers who could carry on the ministry while he proceeded to other opportunities. In this way he was able to multiply and expand his efforts manyfold. He was able to develop increasingly effective ministries wherever he went.

Confidence

Workers have a natural reticence about turning over their ministries to those who are unseasoned or younger. If older, more experienced workers are not careful, they can reflect a no-confidence attitude toward the newer, young worker. Paul was aware of that tendency, so he told the Corinthian church to show Timothy the respect and trust he deserved and badly needed: "See to it that he has nothing to fear while he is with you." And again, "No one . . . should refuse to accept him. Send him on his way in peace."

One of the most important principles in training effective workers is what I call confidence-building.

The importance of enlisting and developing workers was first impressed on me by Dawson Trotman, founder of the Navigators. In April, 1956, Donna and I were missionary appointees preparing to leave for Vietnam. Our mission leaders sent us to Park Street Church in Boston, where Trotman was one of the key speakers. The truth which he emphasized and which most captivated my attention was that Christians—most especially missionaries—are born to reproduce. Christ didn't send us to make decisions but to make disciples. My task as a missionary was not over when I was used of God to win people to Christ and integrate them into the church. I must also reproduce myself in those converts. They, too, must become effective witnesses for Christ.

In Robert Coleman's book, *The Master Plan of Evangelism,* I found the method I needed in order to reproduce myself. Coleman pointed out that in the midst of His evangelism, Jesus Christ was constantly preparing future workers. He did it with on-the-job training. That is, He selected 12 disciples and kept them with Him wherever he went. They could observe

Him, hear what He had to say, follow His example, catch His passion for lost people, learn from Him how to win people, experience firsthand how He made disciples.

Dad also had good advice for me. "Tom," he would say, "don't ever underestimate the dedication, ability and potential of the Vietnamese workers with whom you serve. Believe in them, love them, train them, cooperate wholeheartedly with them. And when the time is right, turn the work over to them."

Dad had already done exactly what he advised me to do. In 1949 he and Mom were assigned to church planting in Saigon. At the time, the church had but one congregation in a town or city, no matter how large the community. To have more than one church in a given place could only mean a church split!

Dad assured the church he had no intention of splitting the existing church in Saigon. He would start a brand-new congregation a considerable distance from the already existing, large Saigon church. But he would ask them to help in one way. He needed a coworker to assist him and to give continuity to the new church when it came time for Dad to move on.

Still opposed to the idea of more than one church in Saigon, the leaders grudgingly acceded to Dad's request. They assigned him the weakest worker they had. Dad graciously received the man, expressing confidence in him, delegating responsibility to him. To the surprise of everyone but Dad, the pastor responded enthusiastically, developing into an outstanding worker. The new church he and Dad planted became one of the strongest in the district.

D. James Kennedy's book, *Evangelism Explosion,* was the next invaluable tool to help me train workers. Dawson Trotman and Robert Coleman gave me the vision and the motivation to equip workers through on-the-job training. James Kennedy gave me the tool that increased my effectiveness many-fold.

While I was ministering in Hong Kong, a seminary student, Young Man Chan, asked if he could be my intern for the summer.

"Yes," I replied, "—if you'll let me set the agenda!"

"What will it be?" he inquired.

"It's called 'EE,' " I explained. "There will be classes and homework, but, most important of all, on-the-job training in evangelism and discipleship."

When I began mentoring Young Man Chan, I knew I had a diamond in the rough. But I didn't realize that one day he would be not only a successful pastor but the leader for Evangelism Explosion among all the Chinese of the world and an interpreter for Billy Graham during his Hong Kong crusade.

In Hong Kong and later in Omaha, I determined that mentoring young men would continue to be an integral part of my ministry. My first tool has been Evangelism Explosion, for four main reasons:

1. Jesus' first course for workers was on-the-job training in fishing for men.

2. Sharing one's faith seems to be the first step in discovering other areas of giftedness and ministry. Paul wrote to Philemon, "I pray that you may be active in sharing your faith, so that you will have a full understanding of every good thing we have in Christ" (Philemon 6).

3. Equipping Christians to share their faith across the street prepares them to share their faith cross-culturally or across the sea.

4. The on-the-job training of EE gives Christians a model for training their future fellow workers not only in evangelism but in other areas of ministry as well.

Let me encourage you to follow Christ's example of training workers. Sending them off to Bible college or seminary is important. But in addition, it is important that they have on-the-job training. If you don't know how to give this to them, let me suggest that you attend an EE clinic and follow the procedures you will learn there. Paul said to Timothy, "The things you have heard me say in the presence of many witnesses entrust to reliable men who will also be qualified to teach others" (2 Timothy 2:2).

Another tool I have found very helpful in developing workers is Bobb Biehl's *Masterplanning*. Biehl builds on the principles I learned from Trotman, Coleman and Kennedy. His leadership and administrative pointers have enabled me to enlist, train and delegate ministry to gifted church laypeople. This, in turn, has freed me to be more effective in my work.

Still Work to Be Done

Many suppose that with the emergence of strong indigenous churches in most lands, the day of foreign missions is passing. Until Jesus returns, missionaries will be needed. Did not Jesus predict, "This gospel of the kingdom will be preached in the whole world as a testimony to all nations, and then the end will come" (Matthew 24:14)? As long as there are unreached people, there will be a need for missionaries.

I see two principal roles for today's missionaries: (1) penetrating unreached people groups and (2) acting as catalysts within the younger churches.

There are still hundreds and hundreds of unreached people groups where no church has been planted, where little or no evangelism is taking place. Some are large blocks of people—for example, Islamic nations with little or no Christian witness. Some are smaller groups—perhaps upper-class people within an urban setting or ethnic minorities within a nation. Until there are witnessing converts among them, they can be reached only from the outside, cross-culturally.

What is a catalyst? It is an element outside a chemical reaction that accelerates that reaction. So a missionary is a foreigner who, from outside the existing church, can accelerate the church's evangelism and discipleship process. For example, earlier I mentioned the opposition from the Vietnamese church when my father first proposed a second congregation in Saigon. By the time Dad had planted his fourth and fifth churches in the city, the church leaders who had opposed him saw the great benefits. They themselves took hold of the idea and went on to plant 40 churches in Saigon!

Today, as in Paul's day, great doors for effective work are open to missionaries on every continent. Jesus declares that "what he opens no one can shut" (Revelation 3:7). He holds the keys! May we enter those wide-open doors while people are responsive. May we effectively do the work that God commands us to do.

Study Guide Questions

1. What is the difference between being *efficient* and being *effective*? How does the distinction apply to the missionary? How does it apply to you?

2. Should missionaries be reticent about making known to their constituents the financial needs of their work? In what ways might churches at home aid the work of their missionaries?

3. What does it mean to give responsibly to God's work? What checks and balances are necessary to assure such responsibility? Have you investigated to be sure your missionary dollars are being used wisely?

4. What do difficulties and opposition often signal? What should be the missionary's response? What should be the response of homeland Christians?

5. What three vital issues were involved in Paul's recruiting of fellow workers? What is the implication of these issues for missions?

6. With strong indigenous churches in most third world nations, what two remaining ministries especially fit the missionary?

Endnotes
1. *Our Daily Bread* (Grand Rapids, MI: Radio Bible Class), July, 1992.

Chapter Eight

Mountains, Mustard Seed and Miracles

Matthew 17

MOUNTAINS FASCINATE ME! Their sheer size, permanence and beauty leave me in breathless awe and wonder. But above all, they turn my thoughts to God.

On our way to and from Vietnam, Donna and I have visited exotic countries. Like other travelers, we have been drawn to a wide variety of tourist attractions. But one of our most pervasive impressions has been the pride these countries take in their mountains.

Driving across the United States we passed majestic Mount Hood in Oregon. Flying over Japan, we gasped in awe as Mount Fuji came into view. From the Red Sea we photographed—in the distance—Mount Sinai of Old Testament renown. By train we traveled through the gorgeous snowcapped Alps of northern Italy and Switzerland. After an evening of prayer in Seoul, Korea, an OMS missionary took us to the city's top tourist spot—a mountain! Whatever the continent, people take pride in their mountains.

In the Scriptures mountains figure prominently. The ark rested on Mount Ararat. Abraham learned faith on Mount Moriah. God delivered the law to Israel on Mount Sinai. Jesus' best-known discourse was His Sermon on the Mount (Matthew 5-7). He ascended from and will return to the Mount of Olives.

In Matthew 17 we have a real mountain and two figurative mountains. The real mountain was the mount of Jesus' transfiguration. Since Jesus and His disciples had been in the region of Caesarea Philippi a week earlier (Matthew 16:13, 17:1), many suppose it was Mount Hermon, a prominent, usually snowcapped peak northeast of that inland city. Peter was among the select three disciples who accompanied Jesus up the mount of transfiguration. Peter also plays a part when it comes to the two figurative mountains we will look at.

Peter is my favorite Bible character. I can't identify with Paul; he was too outstanding. With Peter I feel comfortable! He had his ups and downs, his hots and colds, his moments of great faith and relapses into doubt. He was intensely human. He knew frustration, anxiety, temptation—just like most of us!

Jesus' words in Matthew 17:20 will be our key text for this chapter of *Missions by the Book*:

> I tell you the truth, if you have faith as small as a mustard seed, you can say to this mountain, 'Move from here to there' and it will move. Nothing will be impossible for you.

Jesus referred to one of the largest objects the human eye can see, a mountain, and to one of the smallest objects the human eye can see, a mustard seed. He told His disciples that God, who specializes in doing the impossible, stands between the two, ready to work miracles. The condition, the secret, the key—call it what you want—was *faith!*

Faith is basic to the Christian life. The Bible tells us so. We are saved by faith (John 3:16). We live by faith (Galatians 2:20). We pray in faith, we witness in faith, we are to die in faith (see Hebrews 11:13). "Without faith it is impossible to please God" (Hebrews 11:6). "Everything that does not come from faith is sin" (Romans 14:23).

But what is faith? It is a certain trust in the invisible God (Hebrews 11:1-3). It is a gift from God (Ephesians 2:8). Unbelievers are inclined to regard faith as a crutch without which emotionally disturbed people can't make it through life.

Others equate it with superstition. They suppose to exercise faith means to kiss all reason good-bye.

In his daily devotional, *Renewed Day by Day*, A.W. Tozer distinguishes faith from superstition:

> Real faith is not the stuff dreams are made of; rather it is tough, practical and altogether realistic. Faith sees the invisible but it does not see the nonexistent. . . .
>
> Faith is not a noble quality found only in superior men. It is not a virtue attainable by a limited few. It is not the quality to persuade ourselves that black is white or that something we desire will come to pass if we only wish hard enough. Faith is simply the bringing of our minds into accord with truth. It is adjusting our expectations to the promises of God in complete assurance that the God of the whole earth cannot lie![1]

All of us commit ourselves to the unseen. Almost daily we trust invisible reality. We make promises over the phone to people we can't see. We ride in planes held up by invisible air and piloted by people hidden from view. We eat food prepared by chefs we never meet. We accept and deposit checks with confidence that behind-the-scenes bank personnel will credit our accounts with the money. We drive at night trusting the indiscernible driver behind the approaching headlights to keep his or her car on the right side of the road. Why, then, is it so difficult to trust the invisible God who through the centuries has proven Himself to be utterly trustworthy?

But let's return to Peter and our study of faith. In the region of Caesarea Philippi, Peter made his great *profession* of faith: "You are the Christ, the Son of the living God" (Matthew 16:16). Peter heard Jesus declare the *price* of faith: "If anyone would come after me, he must deny himself and take up his cross and follow me" (Matthew 16:24). And in Matthew 17:20 Peter learned the *proof* of faith—mountains that move miraculously!

What I think Jesus was saying to Peter was this: "You have trusted in Me by faith and you have taken up your cross to follow Me by faith. Now you're going to encounter tests of your faith. You'll meet up with some impossible situations that will be like mountains to you. You will be faced with some unbearable trials, some unexpected emergencies, some tremendous needs. You will encounter some unparalleled opportunities, some unavoidable impasses.

"Like mountains, you'll find you cannot get around these things or cross over them or tunnel through them. Your only solution will be to turn to your mountain-moving God and say in faith, 'Mountain, move!' And though your faith may be as small as a mustard seed, if it's in the almighty, miracle-working God, He will do the impossible! He will move your mountains."

Missionaries, too, encounter mountains! Just like Peter and the other disciples, they must live and labor in faith. *Faith is absolutely essential for the missionary who would live triumphantly and work effectively.*

As a missionary in Vietnam, I found Peter's experiences, as recorded in Matthew 17, to be both edifying and encouraging. By faith in God I could handle those insurmountable mountains. And so can you!

Let's look at these three mountains that tested Peter's faith. The first was . . .

1. A Physical Mountain

After six days Jesus took with him Peter, James and John the brother of James, and led them up a high mountain by themselves. (Matthew 17:1)

Notice that this first mountain Peter encountered was real. It was a real physical mountain of earth, rocks, trees, streams and whatever else comprised that mountain. Matthew notes that it was high. If indeed it was Mount Hermon, it towered some 9,000 feet above sea level.

I suggest that when Christ asked Peter, James and John to climb that mountain, He was asking them to go where they didn't want to go.

Those three were fishermen. I ministered on Guam for a year among fishermen. Fishermen don't particularly like mountains. Their locale is the sea or the seashore. They never climb mountains.

So I can't help but imagine that when Jesus asked Peter and his two ex-fishermen colleagues to go mountain climbing, they were a bit taken back. I can almost hear Peter protesting, "But, Lord, there are no fish up there! There are no people up there!" And as his muscles began to ache and perspiration drenched his tunic and his feet began to blister, he was tempted to complain. If Peter ever needed faith, it was then.

But I want you to notice something amazing. When Peter trusted His Lord and went with Him to the place he didn't want to go, Christ blessed him beyond words. The place Peter didn't want to go became the place he didn't want to leave.

> Peter said to Jesus, "Lord, it is good for us to be here. If you wish, I will put up three shelters—one for you, one for Moses and one for Elijah." (17:4)

Peter wasn't even worried about himself. He and his companions could brave the sun, the wind and the rain. They could even sleep under the stars if only they might stay in the place to which Christ had brought them.

It's amazing how Christ can change people's attitudes. Situations they would normally dread become situations in which they delight! What changed Peter's attitude about the mountain? I suggest three things.

A Vision

Peter saw the glory of Christ as he had never seen it before. Jesus' countenance "shone like the sun" and His clothing "became as white as the light" (17:2). Some artists portray Christ with a halo. But Christ had no halo over his head. He had laid aside His heavenly glory. Peter, James and John had never before seen His glory, a glory brighter than the noonday sun! Can you imagine Peter's ecstasy? Can you guess what a thrill it must have been to James and John?

A Visit

Peter and friends met some notable visitors: "Just then there appeared before them Moses and Elijah, talking with Jesus" (17:3). Every Jewish boy grew up hearing stories of those two great heroes of the faith. Moses had led God's people from Egyptian captivity to the promised land. He had delivered to them God's written covenant and God's law. Elijah was the prophet who defied the wicked Jezebel. He had prayed down fire. He had prayed down drought-breaking rain. Who would have supposed that climbing a mountain by faith

would lead to such a marvelous rendezvous?
And then there was . . .

A Voice

It was the voice of God the Father saying,
"This is my Son, whom I love; with him I am
well pleased. Listen to him!" (17:5). The three
disciples doubtless had read God's Word from
their youth. But to hear God speaking directly
from heaven in articulated words? Only once
before had it happened, and the message then
was very similar. It was at Jesus' baptism (Matthew 3:16-17), and probably the three disciples
were not present.

The disciples "fell facedown to the ground,
terrified. But Jesus came and touched them.
'Get up,' he said. 'Don't be afraid' " (17:6-7).
Matthew reports: "When they looked up, they
saw no one except Jesus" (17:8).

Really, it was Jesus who turned the mount of
trial into a mount of blessing. He it was who
changed the dreadful place Peter didn't want
to go into the delightful place he didn't want to
leave.

What does all this have to do with missions?
Very much! Take my own situation, for example. I didn't want to go to Vietnam as a missionary. I remembered Vietnam as the land of
boils, mosquitoes, malaria, unbearable heat, un-
pleasant odors and prolonged separation from
family and friends. Many people think missionaries' kids (MKs) have a natural tug to return to

the country of their birth and childhood. I suppose some of them do. But not this MK! Yet when God called me into His service and clearly led Donna and me to Vietnam, He also gave us a love for the people and the work. Twenty years later, I didn't want to leave!

One of my assignments in Vietnam was Danang, on the central coast—a city where I didn't want to go. It was the city where missionary work in Vietnam had begun. The church in Danang was already firmly established. The province had more churches than anywhere else in Vietnam.

But as I prayed about Danang, God reminded me that the church in Danang, although the oldest, was the *only* Protestant church for a population of 200,000. In fact, there was a desperate need for more churches in Danang.

As I said earlier, our church leaders resisted the idea of multiple churches in a town or city. The plan had worked in Saigon, but Saigon was huge compared with Danang. Even as I prayed, God put upon the heart of the Danang pastor, Le dinh To, the desire to plant more churches in the city. Unfortunately, his church leaders had not yet caught the same vision. They didn't see how a town of only 200,000 could support a second church. Pastor To and I knew it would be unwise to begin without their cooperation. So we prayed together weekly that God would change their minds.

Pastor To invited me to take over the Bible study at the Tuesday evening prayer meetings. Systematically I went through the Book of Acts. In every chapter I found evangelism and church extension! Meanwhile, Pastor To and I continued to pray. Before long, one of the church leaders, Vo-ngoc-Ky, was likewise convinced of the need for more churches in Danang. And the three of us met weekly to pray that God would give the other leaders the vision He had given us.

After a year and a half of such prayer and teaching, Pastor To said he felt the time had come for us to make plans. He called a special meeting of the church board to present the matter. He asked me to stay next door and pray!

About halfway through the evening, there was a knock on the door. It was Pastor To.

"Can you come quickly?" he asked. "We need your help. We are in a terrible argument!"

"What's the problem?" I wanted to know.

"There are two factions," Pastor To explained. "One group wants to plant a church at An-Hai, across the river. The other insists the best place is at Hai-Chau, near the airport."

"That's a wonderful problem!" I exclaimed. "It means we can plant *two* new churches instead of one!"

As I met with the two animated factions, I suggested that the group first to find land we would help with a building. In the other area, we would rent a meeting place. My proposal motivated both groups to move quickly. Within a year we had two new churches, well attended with new people coming to Christ. And the mother church, to everyone's surprise, continued to grow. A surplus of income enabled the congregation to enlarge the sanctuary to accommodate all the new people being saved! The place I didn't want to go again became the place I didn't want to leave.

Has God put you in a place you never wanted to be? Has He given you a ministry you would never have chosen for yourself? Are you about to be sent to what, in your assessment, is an undesirable place? Talk to God about it. If He assures you it is the place or the work He wants for you, trust Him and accept His direction. God will surprise you over and over by revealing to you His glory, speaking to you through His Word, bringing you into contact with some very wonderful people that you might not otherwise have met. He did it for Peter. He did it for me. He can transform your place of dread into a place of delight. His presence will make your prison a palace!

2. A Family Mountain

Peter wanted to stay indefinitely on that mountain with Jesus. Jesus had other plans. As He led His three disciples "down the mountain" (17:9), Peter may have thought he was through with mountains for a while. But we read in 17:14 that they came to a crowd of people. Within that gathering of humanity was a family. The family had a mountain of a problem. The mountain needed to be moved.

A man approached Jesus and knelt before him. "Lord, have mercy on my son," he said. "He has seizures and is suffering greatly. He often falls into the fire or into the water. I brought him to your disciples, but they could not heal him."

"O unbelieving and perverse generation," Jesus replied, "how long shall I stay with you? How long shall I put up with you? Bring the boy here to me." Jesus rebuked the demon, and it came out of the boy, and he was healed from that moment.

Then the disciples came to Jesus in private and asked, "Why couldn't we drive it out?"

He replied, "Because you have so little faith. I tell you the truth, if you have faith as small as a mustard seed, you can say to this mountain, 'Move from here to there' and it will move. Nothing will be impossible for you." (17:14-21)

How many times Satan attacks our families with one trial after another! Like the disciples, when we trust in our own resources, we utterly fail to move the mountains. But if in simple faith we will bring our problems to Jesus, He will do the miraculous. He will move mountains for our families.

Missionary families, of course, are not exempt from mountainous problems. As we serve God overseas, we will encounter satanic attacks upon our homes.

In 1964, Donna and I were living in Hue, Vietnam. At that time we had three children: nine-year-old Jennifer, five-year-old Jeff and four-year-old John. Jennifer felt outnumbered, and the two boys agreed that a baby sister would be a good idea. But the baby had to be a girl! The children began to pray.

One happy day, Donna announced that, sure enough, a baby was on the way! Our Vietnamese doctor told us the baby would have to be delivered by cesarean section, as our two boys had been. He set March 10, 1966, as the day. That morning, I discovered that the potted rosebush I had given Donna for Christmas had sprouted its first bud—and the bud was pink! When I reentered the house to announce this omen, I found Donna dressed in a pink housecoat, setting the table with a pink cloth and pink melmac dishes.

"Sweetheart," I exclaimed, "I think all the signs point to a girl today!"

March 10, 1966, turned out to be momentous in another way. It was the day Air Marshall Nguyen cao Ky, the top leader in Saigon, fired General Nguyen chanh Thi, the commanding general for all the troops in Central Vietnam. General Thi's home was just a few doors from ours. Indeed, he had become a personal friend. He was a highly respected hero and leader in central Vietnam. When the news of his firing hit the wires, bedlam broke out. Demonstrators marched down the main streets of Hue. Buddhist priests dragged their altars and images into the streets. Several priests burned themselves to death in protest. Just over our backyard wall, other extremists broke down the doors of the U.S. Information Center and tossed computers, projectors, typewriters, TVs and furniture out the windows.

At the hospital Janice Esther, the girl we all had been hoping for, put in her appearance on schedule. But when the two doctors who had delivered her were later examining her in the nursery, I sensed a problem. One doctor was pulling and pushing her legs. He shook his head and whispered something to the other man.

"We're sorry, Missionary," he apologized to me. "Your wife had a ruptured ovary, and we were concerned about the baby. Being in a hurry, we pulled too hard and broke your daughter's leg. You can be sure we'll do everything possible for your wife and child."

A few days later they brought a specialist who put the leg in traction. To keep the broken limb straight, they built a brace about 30 inches high that extended her legs straight up. That is how Janice came home from the hospital.

Lying in that unnatural position 24 hours a day was extremely uncomfortable. It also produced a deep ulcer on her back. Infection caused her temperature to rise alarmingly. We called in a German pediatrician teaching in the Hue University School of Medicine. We did not know he was recovering from a 20-day coma and was in no condition to treat Janice. He experimented with some free new antibiotic samples, giving our baby adult dosages. This and an unnecessarily strong milk formula caused an intestinal blockage. It was back to the hospital for Janice.

Nursing care in Vietnam was far from American standards of sanitation. But my sister Harriette Irwin had come to assist during Donna's delivery and recovery. And the political turmoil kept a Wycliffe nurse, Pat Bonnell, from returning to her post. These two women volunteered to provide 24 hour American nursing care for our critically ill cherub.

As Janice's condition went from bad to worse, she was put in an incubator and fed through tubes. Her weight dropped from eight pounds to less than five. I knew she could not survive much longer. We had exhausted every medical possibility.

At about 2 a.m. one night, unable to sleep, I was reading Exodus 15. I came to the last part of verse 26: "I am the LORD, who heals you." Immediately I bowed my head in prayer.

"Lord," I prayed, "forgive me! I have been placing my trust in doctors when all along You are the One who alone can heal. I ask You to work a miracle and save the life of my child." The next day I sent an urgent cablegram to Donna's mother, Mable Stadsklev, asking her to request prayer wherever she could. Mother went to work, and soon women's prayer groups across America were praying for little Janice's recovery.

That was the turning point. Janice herself reached up with her weak little hand and pulled out the stomach tube that had been keeping her alive. When Harriette, my sister, offered her a bottle of milk, she began sucking on the nipple as if her life depended on it—and it did!

Our trauma was not over, however. The political situation worsened. It became so serious that the U.S. military asked all Americans to leave Hue. And Janice was still in the hospital, still critically ill. We took her direct from the hospital to the helipad, sponging her to keep her temperature normal in the hot, midday sun, then fearing she would catch her death of cold as the chopper gained altitude over the Ai Van mountain pass between Hue and Danang.

God was good to us. Janice suffered no ill effects from the trip. Evacuated with us was a German doctor who had nothing to do for the next month except to take care of Janice. Sailors at the naval base where we were housed entertained our two boys with fire engine rides, films about a cross-eyed lion and a makeshift playground which they put together for the great occasion of entertaining American civilian families!

By the time we were permitted to return to Hue, Janice had regained her birth weight and was flourishing. Back in Hue, I made a point to find the two Vietnamese doctors. I thanked them for all their care. Because of socialized medicine, their services had been no direct expense to us. To show my gratitude, I bought each one a chicken and a large ham.

Both were surprised by my overture. "Why do you thank us?" one doctor responded. "We made mistakes." Then pointing his index finger heavenward he added, "You must thank your God! He's the One who saved your child's life, not us! Your child is alive today because of a miracle!"

Coming from a Buddhist, that was quite a testimony! Through mustard seed-sized faith we saw our miracle-working God move a mountain.

3. A Financial Mountain

Returning to our Scripture in Matthew 17, we find that Peter is about to face one more insurmountable mountain. He has descended the mountain he thought he did not want to climb. He has watched as Jesus, by His miraculous power, removed the mountain that faced the distraught family seeking the Master's help.

Now Peter faces what I will call a financial mountain.

> After Jesus and his disciples arrived in Capernaum, the collectors of the two-drachma tax came to Peter and asked, "Doesn't your teacher pay the temple tax?"
>
> "Yes, he does," he replied.
>
> When Peter came into the house, Jesus was the first to speak. "What do you think, Simon?" he asked. "From whom do the kings of the earth collect duty and taxes—from their own sons or from others?"
>
> "From others," Peter answered.
>
> "Then the sons are exempt," Jesus said to him. "But so that we may not offend them, go to the lake and throw out your line. Take the first fish you catch; open its mouth and you will find a four-drachma coin. Take it and give it to them for my tax and yours." (17:24-27)

Pressing Need

Even Jesus and His disciples could not do without a certain amount of money. In this case, it was money to pay their tax assessments. Jesus would later make His well-known pronouncement about giving to Caesar what is Caesar's (Matthew 22:21).

Clearly, Jesus was on the side of responsibility to government.

But where was the money to come from? For our sakes Jesus had become poor. He had left His heavenly riches. Earlier he had re-marked to a would-be follower, "Foxes have holes and birds of the air have nests, but the Son of Man has no place to lay his head" (Matthew 8:20). Nor did Peter have the four drachma. He had left his fishing business—his boat and his nets—in order to follow Je-sus. Peter had given up his livelihood. Now he was face-to-face with another mountain—a financial mountain!

Personal Involvement

Jesus was about to work another miracle. He was about to move another of Peter's moun-tains. But we need to see something very im-portant. Jesus did not intend to supply the need without Peter's participation. In fact, He was going to use Peter's vocational skill as part of that miracle. When Peter would do his part, obediently, believingly, Jesus would add His miracle. God will do for us the things we can-not do for ourselves, but He will not do for us the things we *can* do.

Fishing was one thing Peter could do, and do well. So Jesus told Peter to catch a fish. I can al-most see Peter's smile as Jesus bade him go fishing. Peter may not have liked to climb mountains, but he loved to fish! He had fished from childhood. So off to the shore Peter went to use his angling skills, to do his part.

At the beginning of chapter 6 of this book, I related some of the jobs I worked at in order to put myself through college. I recall only two times when God miraculously supplied my financial needs. Both times, I had first done what I could—just like Peter did.

One morning as I was dressing for class I was chagrined to discover I was putting on my last set of clean clothes. The rules forbade doing laundry in the bathroom. The coin-operated washers required 15 cents, and I was penniless. On principle, I refused to borrow money from anyone. My next payday was not until the end of the week. If anyone faced a financial mountain, I was the one at that moment!

I did what any Christian should do. I prayed. In very simple terms I asked God for 15 cents! Then I went to breakfast and from there to classes.

Following classes, I walked down the hill to Reliable Market, where I drove a red panel truck delivering groceries. For whatever reason, the store's customers were not in the habit of tipping. Each time I carried groceries into a home, the person would give me the exact amount of the bill. But that day one of the customers paid me for her groceries, saying, "There may be a few extra pennies left over. If so, you keep them, OK?"

Back in the truck, I counted the money again.

Sure enough, there were some "extra pennies"—15 extra pennies! At the market I exchanged those 15 pennies for a dime and a nickel. And when work was finished, I practically ran up the hill to do my laundry. I doubt that $15,000 would have meant any more to me right then than those 15 pennies which God supplied to meet my immediate need! That day I learned that childlike faith can move financial mountains.

Pleasant Surprise

That brings us to another lesson from Peter's urgent need and personal involvement. Jesus didn't ask Peter to get into a boat and, by means of a net, pull in a great number of fish. He didn't ask Peter to market his catch, expecting that the sale would yield the needed four drachmas. No. Jesus told Peter to go to the lake, throw in a line and catch one fish! In the mouth of that one fish would be the necessary money for the temple tax owed by Jesus and Peter.

Peter easily could have argued with the Lord. Jesus' trade was carpentry, not fishing. Peter had been fishing for a living all his adult life. He had caught thousands and thousands of fish. Not once had he discovered money in their mouths! But Peter did not argue. He didn't question the Lord's instructions, ridiculous though they must have seemed to him. He simply took his line and hook down to the lake and threw them out for the catch. That had to be one of Peter's greatest moments. Obedience, no questions asked!

God rewarded Peter's trust. Just as Jesus said, Peter found in the mouth of his first catch the money he and Jesus needed, no more, no less.

God loves to supply our urgent financial needs in surprising ways! He has sources of supply where we least expect them. We pray and then strategize how we think God should meet those needs. But in His own time and way, and for His own glory, God moves financial mountains.

Priority Order

There is one other detail that we need to note. The money would pay Jesus' tax and Peter's. Note the order. God is always to be first in our finances. We are to give Him the first day of the week, the firstfruits of our labor. We are to seek first His kingdom and His righteousness.

As a freshman in college, I made it a point to put God first in money matters. I had made a "faith promise" for missions. Every month I had pledged to give a specified amount. When I received a paycheck, I first gave toward my missions faith promise. Then I would pay my college bills and care for other incidentals.

It was after the summer I worked in Iowa that God, for the second time, provided money miraculously for me. I had covenanted with God to give Him the tithe of all I earned. I calculated that if I lived and ate frugally, I should be able to do that and still have what I needed for my tuition. My frugality that summer cost me some pounds. But God blessed me mightily as I learned to give sacrificially and first-of-all to Him. I wouldn't exchange the experience for anything!

To my great surprise, however, when I went to pay my college tuition, I was $10 short. I can't fully describe my disappointment. Hadn't I done my part? Hadn't I skimped almost beyond reason to save enough for school expenses? Hadn't I kept God first in my financial matters? How could this happen to me?

As I stood there in the college office, red-faced, trying to decide what to do, the accountant checked the records again.

"Sorry, Tom," she exclaimed apologetically. "Someone came in earlier and deposited $10 to your account. You're all paid up!" What joy flooded my heart!

As I think back on the incident, I see the same pattern that Peter experienced. I had a *pressing need.* I was *personally involved,* working all summer to do my part in meeting the need. I followed God's *priority order,* giving the tithe to God first. God responded by giving me a *pleasant surprise,* supplying the balance of my need from an unexpected source.

At the physical mountain where Jesus was transfigured, Peter trusted His Lord on uncomfortable terrain. When he faced the family mountain—the demon-possessed boy—Peter learned to trust Jesus' unfathomable power. Before the financial mountain, he discovered an unexpected purse. Each was a lesson in faith, lessons invaluable for every missionary and every missions-minded believer.

At the first mountain is the lesson of *going*—going in faith and obedience wherever God sends us. At the second mountain is the lesson of *praying*—until God does the impossible as we commit to Him our families and our critical needs. At the third mountain is the lesson of *giving*—entrusting to Him our finances, both our investments in His work and the income necessary for our needs.

How wonderful to live, to walk and to serve God in faith! When we do, we will see our mountains of trial become mountains of transfiguration. We will see God glorified in marvelous and miraculous ways.

Are you facing insurmountable mountains? Read Matthew 17 again and learn from Peter how to handle the mountains!

There's an old chorus that I dearly love. As a missionary I sang it over and over. Its promise still applies.

> Got any rivers you think are
>   uncrossable?
>   Got any mountains you cannot
>   tunnel through?

God specializes in things thought
impossible.
He'll do for you what no other one
can do!

Study Guide Questions

1. How important is faith to a Christian's life and ministry? List areas where faith is especially important.

2. How would you equate Peter's three mountains (Matthew 17) with a present-day missionary's life and ministry?

3. What transformed Peter's "mountain of trial" into a "mountain of blessing"? How might it apply to missionary service? How might it apply to you?

4. What unseen spiritual force was responsible for the "family mountain" (Matthew 17:14-23)? How might this apply to missionary families today? How might it apply to you?

5. What role did faith play in Peter's dealing with his "financial mountain" (Matthew 17:24-27)? What lessons do you see here for a missionary with financial needs? What lessons do you see for yourself?

6. Why does God seem so often to supply our needs from least expected sources? What part may we have in His provision?

7. What mountains are confronting you? Do you believe God can move them? How will you go about asking Him to do so?

Endnotes

1. Tozer, A.W. *Renewed Day by Day* (Camp Hill, PA: Christian Publications.) February 9 and August 4 readings.

Chapter Nine

The Most You Can Do

James 1-5

MY BROTHER-IN-LAW, DAVID MOORE, then a mis-sionary to Indonesia, was preparing to return overseas following a year in the United States. At the close of a church service in which he spoke, a woman approached him.

"Mr. Moore," the woman said, "as you return to Indonesia, the least I can do is to pray for you."

David, never at a loss for words, responded without hesitation. "Ma'am," he said, "praying for me isn't the *least* you can do; it's the *most* you can do!"

My brother-in-law was right. *There is nothing more needed, more powerful, more influential in missionary work than prayer.* That is the thesis of this chapter.

I've often said it. No prayer, no blessing. Little prayer, little blessing. Much prayer, much

blessing. Volumes of prayer, people move-
ments, whole communities turning to God, revival fires sweeping through the church. A
book with the title this one bears would be in-
complete without at least one chapter devoted
to prayer by the Book.

The Bible, of course, has much to say about
prayer. We could turn many places within its
pages for instruction on praying. But throughout this book, I've shared the Scriptures that
most deeply impacted my missionary ministry.
With that in mind, I turn to the little Letter of
James for instruction on prayer. Through the
years, James has become my "prayer book."

What really got me started examining James
for instruction on prayer was one of my Grandfather Hartman's letters to my mother, his
daughter. As I mentioned, John Hartman was a
missionary to the Caribbean. Years later, he
wrote much thoughtful spiritual counsel to my
parents in Vietnam. I treasure that two-inch-
high stack of letters. I have read and reread
them carefully.

In one letter Grandpa Hartman referred to a
sermon he had preached from the book of
James. The title: "Why God Doesn't Answer
Prayer." That's all he said. He mentioned no
sermon outline, no specific text, no illustrations
or applications. But the title was enough to
start me perusing James to see what he had to
say about prayer. And as I read, I came to the
big thought that would change my prayer life:

"The prayer of a righteous man is powerful and effective" (5:16).

With that verse in my mind, I began studying the book in earnest, praying as I went, asking God to show me how a person can pray powerfully and effectively. In James' relatively short letter, I found four basic conditions that have shaped my prayer life.

Right up front, let me make one thing clear. I do not purport to be an expert on prayer or even a model for you to follow. Books could be written about all I *don't* know about prayer. But accept, if you will, the four simple keys to effective praying that I learned at the feet of James. I've seen God use them powerfully in my own life and ministry. I believe they will work as effectively for you.

The James who wrote James was almost certainly the half brother of Jesus. James did not become a believer until some time after Jesus' resurrection from the dead. But as a boy and a young man, he would have watched his older Brother commune with God. Even at that time, Jesus was in regular touch with His Father God through prayer. I say that confidently because later on, prayer was Jesus' habit. As Jesus was being baptized, He prayed (Luke 3:21). Before He selected His disciples, He prayed all night (6:12). Just prior to Peter's great confession, Jesus was praying (9:18). At the transfiguration He was praying (9:28). As the 70 returned from ministry, He was praying (10:21). Jesus was praying when His disciples asked Him to teach them to pray (11:1). He prayed as He broke the bread at the last supper (22:19). He prayed in Gethsemane (22:41). He prayed for those crucifying Him (23:34). He prayed as He sacrificed His life on the cross (23:46). Patterns tend to be established early, not suddenly. Prayer was a habit with Jesus, and James would have had opportunity to observe some of its early formation in Jesus' life.

I can't help but think that James must have enjoyed some long discussions with Jesus about prayer. He certainly never forgot Jesus' example. After James became a believer in the resurrected Christ Jesus, he discovered that those conversations of earlier years could continue. Jesus, his elder Brother, was in heaven, but He was accessible through prayer.

Later James became bishop of Jerusalem. The responsibilities of that office must have kept him in frequent touch with Jesus. Tradition has it that James prayed so much that he developed callouses on his knees. In fact, people called him "Old Camel Knees." This praying bishop of Jerusalem saw God do amazing things: When famine threatened the very lives of his members, God used the gifts of "foreign"—Gentile—believers to sustain them (Acts 11:27-30). Angels delivered Peter from Herod's maximum-security prison (Acts 12). The Holy Spirit reconciled a serious difference of opinion that could have split the young church (Acts 15). A second monetary gift from the "mission field" relieved impoverished church members (Acts 21:17-19; 2 Corinthians 8-9). If anyone is qualified to teach us about prayer, certainly it is James!

So let's turn to James' short letter. I see in it four conditions for effective praying. To keep the alliterative pattern we have been using, I have named them *faith, a Father, friendly relations* and *fervency*.

1. Faith

> If any of you lacks wisdom, he should ask God, who gives generously to all without finding fault, and it will be given to him. But when he asks, he must believe and not doubt, because he who doubts is like a wave of the sea, blown and tossed by the wind. That man should not think he will receive anything from the Lord; he is a double-minded man, unstable in all he does. (1:5-8)

Our entire previous chapter dealt with faith and missions: faith to remove physical mountains, family mountains and financial mountains. From my own experiences I shared instances of miraculous answers to prayer. But faith is such a vital part of a missionary's ministry that the subject bears further exploration.

Notice that Jesus refers to prayer as asking God in simple faith for what we lack or need.

Sometimes we make prayer complicated and difficult. In reality, it is so simple that the smallest child can pray. Mustard seed-sized faith is enough to bring God's ready answer. In fact, I have learned much about praying in faith from my four children.

We were living in Hue, Vietnam. Among other things, Hue has the distinction of receiving more than double the rainfall of any other city in Vietnam! The monsoon rains are both heavy and prolonged. Sometimes there is no letup for a month or two. Unfortunately, the monsoon season coincided with our children's school vacation. Thus Donna and I had to look for creative ways to keep the kids occupied and happy indoors.

One vacation, after weeks of rain without a break, Jennifer had a special bedtime petition for God.

"Dear Lord," she prayed, "would you please stop the rain tomorrow and give us a clear, sunny day so we can have a family picnic at the beach?" Donna and I both heard her request. *Jenny*, I thought to myself, *why do you have to be so specific? Why do you have to make it so impossible for God? You don't get sunny weather in the middle of the monsoon season. Furthermore, isn't it a little presumptuous to think God would change the whole weather pattern just so a little girl can have a picnic?* That's what I thought.

It was I who needed the rebuke. The next morning dawned cloudless and sunny. A little child's faith had touched the heart and hand of God! It was as if God had turned off the cosmic spigot just so a little girl's missionary family could have a happy holiday at the beach. And what a happy, praiseful picnic it was! The following day, God turned the faucet back on. The rains returned with a torrential downpour!

When Dr. H.L. Turner, the late president of The Christian and Missionary Alliance, visited Vietnam, he preached in Tuy Hoa about child-like faith. He told how, as a penniless college student, his watch stopped. He had no money to get it repaired. But he remembered that in Bible times, Christ and His apostles laid hands on the sick and they recovered. Young Turner wasn't sure his situation was the same. Nevertheless, he put his hand on his ailing watch and prayed that God would make it work. Some time later, to his great delight, he discovered the watch was running.

Dr. Turner's illustration impressed Pastor Nguyen van Thin. Later, Pastor Thin accepted a call to Banmethuot. One weekday his children were playing in the Banmethuot church when one of them accidentally knocked the clock off the wall. The children owned up to what had happened, but the fact was the clock would not run. And like Dr. Turner, Pastor Thin had no money to get it fixed. Sunday was approaching, when the clock would be needed. Suddenly Pastor Thin recalled Dr. Turner's illustration about his watch.

"Dear Lord," Pastor Thin prayed, "as You healed Dr. Turner's watch back in America, I pray that You will touch this clock for me." He re-hung the clock on the wall and returned to his work.

Shortly, Mrs. Thin went into the church sanctuary and noticed that the clock was not running. She, too, remembered Dr. Turner's story and took the clock down and prayed for it.

Later Pastor Thin passed the clock and noticed to his happy relief that it was ticking. He reset the hands, then ran to announce the miracle to his wife.

"You?" said his wife in surprise. "*I* prayed for that clock!" As they compared notes, they realized that they had both prayed. It was as Jesus promised: "If two of you on earth agree about anything you ask for, it will be done for you by my Father in heaven" (Matthew 18:19).

2. Father

That brings us to the second condition for effective prayer that I see in James' letter:

> Don't be deceived, my dear brothers. Every good and perfect gift is from above, coming down from the Father of the heavenly lights, who does not change like shifting shadows. He chose to give us birth through the word of truth, that we might be a kind of firstfruits of all he created. (1:16-18)

James clearly defines prayer as the opening of our hearts and hands to receive from our heavenly Father the very best of gifts—perfect gifts. Too often we don't realize all that God offers us as Father.

Evangelist J. Wilbur Chapman recounted a testimony given by a man in one of his meetings. Said the man: "I got off at the train depot one day as a tramp. For a year I had begged on the streets. Badly in need of food, I touched a man on the shoulder and said, 'Mister, please give me a dime.' As soon as I saw his face, I recognized my aging father.

" 'Don't you know me?' I asked. Throwing his arms around me, he cried, 'Oh, my son, I have found you at last! All I have is yours!'

"Think of it. I was a tramp who begged for 10 cents from a man I didn't know was my father. Yet for 18 years he had been looking for me to give me all he possessed!"[1]

Sometimes we Christians act more like beggars than sons. Meanwhile, our Father God waits to make available to us all of His richest gifts. Notice three facets of our Father-child relationship with God. First, God is the . . .

Father of the Heavenly Lights

God must be to us neither a Force nor a Formula but our personal, heavenly Father! An impersonal force can do powerful things. But no force can respond appropriately to my individual needs. A mathematical or chemical formula may be logical and predictable. (Too often that is what people expect God to be: logical and predictable.) But no formula perfectly fits my unique situation or best interest. On the other hand, God as Father loves me perfectly, knows my needs perfectly and responds appropriately and perfectly!

One morning Janice, my youngest child, discovered me before the bathroom mirror shaving. She held out her hands for some of the shaving lather, which I gave her without hesitation. She proceeded to apply it to her chin and cheeks. Then she held out her hands for the razor.

As a loving father, I could see that what she was asking for was not good for her. In fact, it was dangerous! So I first removed the blade, then handed the razor to her. It was not exactly what she had in mind, but it was what was best for her. When we pray to God our Father, we can trust Him to give us what is best, what is perfect!

Firstfruits

What do we mean by the word *firstfruits*? In 1:18 James explains that to call God Father, we must first be given "birth through the word of truth, that we might be a kind of firstfruits of all he created." We must experience the new birth. For the first decade of my life I couldn't pray properly because I had not been born again. But since I trusted Christ as Savior and Lord, I have had the privilege of going boldly to God in prayer. I have had the joy of receiving gratefully His good and perfect gifts.

How about you? Do you know God as your Father? Have you, by faith in Christ, become a member of His eternal family? Are you enjoying His good and perfect gifts?

Faithfulness

James says of God that He "does not change like shifting shadows." We live in a changing world full of changing people. We are constantly experiencing personal change. How assuring it is to know that we pray to a God who is unchanging, eternal and dependable! His promises are true and utterly reliable. Heaven and earth will pass away, but our Father God and His Word remain faithful! "Jesus Christ is the same yesterday and today and forever" (Hebrews 13:8).

When in 1964 Donna and I moved to Hue, we were also given responsibility for the Quang-Tri Province to the north, bordering on North Vietnam. In the provincial capital, Quang-Tri City, we had at that time a small group of believers meeting in a rented bookstore. As Pastor Le dinh To and I surveyed the situation, we felt led to pray that God would give us land with good visibility plus enough money to build a church.

Back at Hue, Pastor To and I continued our weekly visits to the military hospital. We distributed wheelchairs and crutches as well as powder and soap to wounded Vietnamese soldiers. One day at the hospital we met Nguyen chanh Thi, the commanding general. He also was visiting the troops bed-to-bed. Because Vietnam was at war, General Thi had both political and military command over Quang-Tri Province and Quang-Tri City. Our ministry to his wounded troops won for us a warm spot in his heart for the gospel.

Pastor To suggested we arrange an appointment with General Thi and apply for a land grant in Quang-Tri City. We made the appointment, and at the set time we were ushered into the general's office. He was surprised that we had no church building in Quang-Tri City.

"The Buddhists have their temples!" he literally shouted. "The Catholics have their churches! And—" he slammed his fist on his desk "—you Protestants will have your land!"

Only a short time later, we received a signed document from the general. He had granted us a piece of land at the fork of Highway One and the main street into the Quang-Tri City. We could not have chosen a better location. Our mission was able to grant us funds for a building, and in a short time we had our church!

There was just one problem. The land on which we built was a former rice field, at least three feet below road level. We had built the church on a high foundation so it actually was above road level. But during the monsoons, the church was like an island in the middle of the sea!

Ngo tan Phi, the local pastor, began praying for a solution. In fact, he spent one whole night on his knees praying that God would somehow send enough fill dirt to bring all the property up to road level. The next morning, an American marine drove up in a military dump truck and asked if he could pray for a while in the church. Quite some time later he emerged. He assured Pastor Phi that things were going to be all right in his life. He thanked the pastor for the solitude the church had afforded him. Then he asked if there was anything tangible he could do to express his appreciation. Was there something he could do to help the pastor and his congregation?

Pastor Phi looked at the dump truck and the sunken former rice paddy surrounding his church building. "Could you fill in the land around my church?" he asked. The marine sped off in a cloud of dust. A few hours later he returned with a load of fill dirt for the church. And behind him was a whole convoy of other dump trucks loaded with dirt! In a few days, those marines had the whole property up to road level!

3. Friendly Relations

It is possible for us to call God *Father* and not be on friendly terms with Him. It is possible that sin has short-circuited our fellowship with

God. No earthly father is likely to shower special benefits upon a son or daughter who is openly disobedient.

The psalmist wrote: "If I had cherished sin in my heart, / the Lord would not have listened" (Psalm 66:18). Isaiah put it this way: "Your iniquities have separated / you from your God; / your sins have hidden his face from you, / so that he will not hear" (Isaiah 59:2).

James speaks of three forces that were damaging his readers' relationship to God in prayer (4:1-10): (a) There was *war* within; (b) They prayed with *wrong motives.; (c) They were worldly.* James called on them to *weep* and *wash* so they might be free from the sin that hindered their prayers. Let's look a little closer at those special points.

There Was War Within

> What causes fights and quarrels among you? Don't they come from your desires that battle within you? You want something but don't get it. You kill and covet, but you cannot have what you want. You quarrel and fight. You do not have, because you do not ask God. (4:1-2)

James is saying that our desires are an army within us, ready at a moment's notice to attack anyone or anything hindering their gratification. If people rush to grab the same thing, they begin to attack each other. Christians are not to fight for what they want; they are to ask God.

They Prayed with Wrong Motives

Part of the problem relates to our motives. Do our desires go beyond what God wants us to have?

> When you ask, you do not receive, because you ask with wrong motives, that you may spend what you get on your pleasures. (4:3)

It is apparent that the prayers of those to whom James was writing had been selfish. They had prayed principally for things that would gratify their selfish desires. They needed to remove themselves from the center of their prayers and focus on God and His will.

They Were Worldly in Their Conduct

James goes even farther, mincing no words in his rebuke of these Christians:

> You adulterous people, don't you know that friendship with the world is hatred toward God? Anyone who chooses to be a friend of the world becomes an enemy of God. (4:4)

James had good reason for the alarm that he sounds. If his readers insisted on being friends with the world, they had, in effect, become enemies of God. God is a jealous lover. He will tolerate no rival.

They Were to Weep and Wash

James knew the only safe course was through confession and repentance.

> Come near to God and he will come near to you. Wash your hands, you sinners, and purify your hearts, you double-minded. Grieve, mourn and wail. Change your laughter to mourning and your joy to gloom. Humble yourselves before the Lord, and he will lift you up. (4:8-10)

James urged his readers to reconciliation with the God they had offended. It was imperative that the friendly relationship they had once experienced with their Father God be restored. Only then would their prayers be heard and answered.

The forces of selfishness and greed and the worldly temptations that sidetracked James' readers are still with us. Missionaries are not immune from them.

In 1969 I became director of The Christian and Missionary Alliance work in Vietnam. By then the war was getting very intense. Each weekday, I began meeting for prayer over the lunch hour with two of my colleagues: Paul Bubna, then pastor of the International Protestant Church in Saigon, and Franklin Irwin.

An effective revivalist of an earlier era had this advice: If you want God to bring revival, draw a circle, kneel within it and pray that God will revive the person in the circle! My two partners and I prayed for personal revival, then for the revival of our fellow missionaries and finally for the revival of the Vietnamese church. After a while, some of our missionaries living on the other side of Saigon and some up in central Vietnam also began to pray for revival. For a year and a half, we prayed.

In 1971 the late William Allen, then pastor in Mansfield, Ohio, accepted our invitation to speak at the annual conference of missionaries. Eighteen years earlier, Pastor Allen had been greatly used of God as a messenger of revival at Nyack College while Donna and I were students there.

But an interesting thing happened. The formal conference was to begin on Sunday with William Allen. On the day before, however, we missionaries gathered for an all-day Saturday prayer meeting. And there and then God began to work in our hearts. As the Holy Spirit moved among us, we began dealing honestly and thoroughly with sin. We made right the differences we had with each other. Missionaries discouraged to the point of quitting found new fervor. One missionary, who admitted he had never in his life led a person to Christ prayed for evangelistic passion. Later, when he spoke at a U.S. servicemen's retreat, a number of the fellows received Christ as their Savior. Pastor Allen's messages during the conference only fanned the flames.

From that conference and the Vietnamese church conference that followed, the revival spread. At the Nhatrang Biblical Theological Institute, Orrel Steinkamp began an elective course on the history of revivals. One student, after presenting his research to the class, fell to his knees, imploring God to send revival to the school and to Vietnam. Before the day was out, the entire student body was on its knees, confessing sin, seeking the filling of the Holy Spirit, finding God.

The revival spread to local churches. Then to Dalat. Then to Banmethuot. Finally to almost the entire tribal highlands area. Churches multiplied as literally tens of thousands turned over their lives to Jesus Christ.

It came when God's people obeyed James' injunction to "wash your hands" and "purify your hearts." It came as they "humbled [themselves] before the Lord."

4. Fervency

"The prayer of a righteous man is powerful and effective." So reads James 5:16 in the New International Version. The still-revered King James Version puts it this way:

> The effectual fervent prayer of a righteous man availeth much.

What is fervent praying? The context of James 5 offers us several illustrations. First James alludes to the farmer who must wait patiently for "the autumn and spring rains." Finally his patience is rewarded as "the land . . . yield[s] its valuable crop" (5:7). James refers to the Old Testament prophets "who spoke in the name of the Lord" (5:10). They persevered, even when people refused to believe them or follow their counsel. Next James alludes to two familiar Old Testament people. One is Job and the other is Elijah. Let's look at these two great men of prayer and see if we can discover what true fervency is.

Job's Perseverance

"You have heard of Job's perseverance," James says, "and have seen what the Lord finally brought about" (5:11). Job was rewarded for his perseverance amid suffering. God brought a happy conclusion to Job's time of testing.

You say, "Job was a super-saint, and I'm just an ordinary person!" Maybe James anticipated your assumption that only people of Job's caliber could pray with fervency and perseverance. So he added another Old Testament saint to the line-up.

Elijah's Earnestness

Notice what he says about Elijah.

Elijah was a man just like us. He prayed earnestly that it would not rain, and it did not rain on the land for three and a half years. Again he prayed, and the heavens gave rain, and the earth produced its crops. (5:17-18)

When we examine the record of Elijah in First Kings 18, we find an interesting contrast between unbiblical fervency and biblical fervency. Elijah was aware of Israel's ambivalence, whether to worship Baal or the Lord God. So he proposed a contest between the prophets of Baal and himself to see whose deity would answer by fire.

The prophets of Baal prayed all morning, shouting and dancing around their altar. Nothing happened. "So they shouted louder and slashed themselves with swords and spears, as was their custom, until their blood flowed. . . . But there was no response, no one answered, no one paid attention" (1 Kings 18:28-29).

There are some yet today who suppose fervent prayer demands shouting or some form of self-torture. If only they cry loudly enough or punish themselves long enough, perhaps their reluctant God will be persuaded to answer their prayers.

When Baal failed to answer, Elijah took his turn. He repaired the Lord's altar and prepared the sacrifice. He even made things as hard as possible for God by thoroughly soaking the sacrifice and the altar with water.

Then Elijah prayed for fire. And God answered so abruptly, so miraculously, so thoroughly that the people "fell prostrate and cried, 'The LORD—he is God! The LORD—he is God!' " (1 Kings 18:39).

But more answered prayer was needed. A three-and-a-half-year drought plagued Israel. What would Elijah do? The prophet climbed to the top of Carmel and knelt on the ground with his face between his knees. On friendly terms with his heavenly Father, Elijah prayed in faith for rain. Not once, but seven times he sent his servant to "look toward the sea" (1 Kings 18:43). The seventh time, the servant reported a small cloud. The answer was on the way!

What was Elijah's secret in prayer? Was it not the same secret as Job's? Patience. Perseverance. Persistence. He continued in prayer with steadfast purpose until he received the answer. Convinced of God's will, he refused to give up until God granted his request.

In April, 1972, a year after the revival broke out in Vietnam, I was in the Philippines. World Vision had invited me to take part in a week-long evangelistic crusade and a pastors' School of Evangelism. As the week came to a close, I received a cable from Vietnam. North Vietnam had launched an all-out invasion across the de-militarized zone. Never until then had the north attempted so bold a move.

I hurried home and arranged with Rev. Doan van Mieng, president of the Vietnamese church, for a joint emergency meeting of our two executive committees. We met at Nhatrang with only one item on our agenda: What should we do in light of the communists' invasion? We prayed for wisdom. We discussed the matter at length. Finally Spencer Sutherland, then teaching at the Theological Institute, suggested we cable Dr. Nathan Bailey, president of The Christian and Missionary Alliance, asking him to call an Alliance world day of prayer.

Dr. Bailey did so. On May 7, Alliance churches across North America and around the world responded as one. And God answered unmistakably. The very next day President Nixon ordered the mining of the Haiphong Harbor, slowing down the flow of arms to the south. Some key generals in the north were reported killed. And for reasons still not known, the armies that had crossed the 17th parallel made an about-face and retreated into the north. It gave us three more years of ministry in Vietnam. And what years they were! Their great fruitfulness surpassed all the previous decades.

James writes about fervent prayer in the context of praying for physical healing.

Is any one of you sick? He should call the elders of the church to pray over him and anoint him with oil in the name of the Lord. And the prayer offered in faith will make the sick person well; the Lord will raise him up. (5:14-15)

During my ministry at Kowloon Tong Alliance Church in Hong Kong, Elder Philip Chan announced sad news. His son Barry had cancer. At the father's request, we anointed and prayed for Barry, but his condition only worsened. It spread from his lymph nodes throughout his body.

Being people of means, the parents took Barry to New York City to one of the world's top-rated cancer treatment centers. Back in Hong Kong, we determined not to give up, but to persist in prayer. In addition to the regular public prayer times and our private times of prayer, we set aside Thursday evenings to pray for Barry's healing.

Meanwhile, in the New York clinic Barry read his Bible, constantly looking for some direction from the Lord. One morning, after the doctor had informed Barry's parents that their son had only a few weeks to live, Barry read these words: "I will not die but live, / and will proclaim what the LORD has done. / The LORD has chastened me severely, / but he has not given me over to death" (Psalm 118:17-18).

It was the promise from God for which Barry had been searching.

"Dad!" Barry fairly shouted. "I've got it! Let's go home to Hong Kong. God is going to heal me!"

When the doctor stopped by, Barry announced the same good news to him. The doctor was skeptical, to say the least. "If your father takes you back to Hong Kong," he warned, "your family will have to assume all responsibility."

With a medical prognosis of only a few weeks to live, father and son figured they had little to lose.

When Barry and his parents arrived in Hong Kong, he looked like walking death. It was difficult for anyone to believe God was going to heal him. But Elder Chan invited all his friends to an evening gathering at his home. He announced to all that Barry had been healed. And sure enough, Barry began to gain strength. Each day he looked a little healthier. Finally, he was the picture of health! Not a trace of cancer remained!

Barry went on to win the tennis championship at the club across the street from our church. He graduated from Wheaton (Illinois) College, then studied medicine at the University of Pennsylvania. Today he is married and the father of two lovely children. God answered prayer. He worked a miracle in answer to persevering, fervent, believing prayer.

It is impossible to emphasize strongly enough the importance of prayer to missions. Everywhere Donna and I have ministered, prayer has been the key. Whatever the type of work, whether evangelizing, teaching, overseeing, pastoring, ministering to refugees, prayer has been the secret of success.

When we prayed, God worked in marvelous ways. When we neglected to pray, God's hand

and blessing were not evident. How important is prayer in *your* life? Do you regularly go to "the throne of grace" to "find grace to help [you] in [your] time of need"? Have you met the Lord at His throne of grace *today*?

My brother-in law, David Moore, was right. Prayer isn't the *least* you can do for missions. It is the *most* you can do. Will you do it? Will you pray? Will you advance the cause of Christ? Will you extend His kingdom around the world through prayer?

Study Guide Questions

1. What is the most significant thing people at the "home base" can do for missionaries? How significant is it?

2. What qualified James to write with such authority about prayer?

3. What are the four conditions for effective praying that James sets forth in his letter?

4. Why might our loving heavenly Father sometimes not grant that for which missionaries on the field or we at home pray? What three hindrances to prayer does James suggest in 4:1-10? How does he suggest we deal with those hindrances?

5. What two Old Testament heroes does James cite in the fifth chapter of his Letter? What strong qualities do they personify?

6. How important is prayer in your life? In what ways are you interceding for God's worldwide missionary advance? In what ways has God answered your prayers? How might you become more effective in prayer?

Endnotes

1. *Our Daily Bread* (Grand Rapids, MI: Radio Bible Class), November, 1992.

Chapter Ten

The High Cost of Missions

Second Samuel 24:18-25

A HOUSEWIFE BOUGHT A BLOUSE IN THE bargain basement of a downtown department store. When she arrived home with her purchase, her husband greeted her with his usual complaint that she was always spending money on clothes.

"But it was marked down from $30 to $15," she countered, "so I saved $15, right?"

"Umm hmm."

"Well," continued the woman brightly, "I bought the blouse with the $15 I saved! So it really cost me nothing."

We can hope the shopper's cooking exceeded her logic, but her conclusion underscores a universal human trait. We want what costs us nothing. We're all looking for the proverbial free lunch. We want, but we don't want to pay!

A country preacher spoke one Sunday morning on the subject, "Eternal Life Is Free!" At the end of the service he announced the usual offering.

One man, on his way out, took issue with the preacher. "Aren't you contradicting yourself, Pastor? You said this morning that salvation is free, and then you asked for an offering!"

"Well, my brother," replied the pastor with a twinkle in his eye, "when you're thirsty, you can go to the river and drink your fill at no cost. The water is free! But when the water is piped into your house, it costs. Likewise eternal life is free, but you have to pay for the piping!"

That, in brief, is the thesis of this chapter. *Eternal life is free, but "piping" it to a needy world costs.* It costs dearly to send missionaries, to print Bibles, to broadcast the good news by radio and TV. Fulfilling the Great Commission is costly.

A fascinating story is tucked away in Second Samuel 24. It's a story that dynamically illustrates this truth that world missions is costly. We want to look at the story, first in broad strokes, and then as we apply it to world missions.

King David had been enjoying unusual success. His military prowess was renown. His political power had increased significantly. The two had caused pride and ambition to fester in his heart. The infection had spread as well to David's people, the nation of Israel.

At first the problems lay below the surface. Outwardly, all seemed well. But then David rashly did something that brought the malaise to a head. In self-aggrandizement over past successes and perhaps ambitious concerning the future, he decided to number Israel and Judah.

The idea of a census was not wrong. Twice under Moses Israel had been numbered. It was David's motive at this time that made the census wrong. He wished to brag about the number of his armed forces and his military might. And God was not pleased. Through Gad the prophet he gave David three options: Three years of famine, three months of military reversals or three days of plague. David judiciously chose plague, preferring to "fall into the hands of the LORD, for his mercy is great" (2 Samuel 24:14). Rather rapidly, God wiped out 70,000 Israelites. He wanted the ambitious king and his people to see that they had been raised up not to be a threat but a light to the nations. David and Israel were caught up in a "numbers game." God wanted them to focus on His purpose for them as a nation.

The plague fulfilled God's design. It got David's attention and led to his repentance. So God sent Gad to David again, this time with a plan to stop the plague and save the nation. Gad instructed David to buy Araunah's threshing floor and build there an altar.

Threshing floors, whenever possible, were laid out on high places where the wind could more easily blow away the chaff and dust. We know from Second Chronicles 3:1 exactly where Araunah's threshing floor was located. It was atop Mount Moriah, the place where Isaac almost became Abraham's sacrifice and where later Solomon would build Israel's temple.

In respect for the king and concerned for his people, Araunah offered David not only his threshing floor, but his oxen, their yokes and his threshing instruments—free of charge. But David refused. He told Araunah, "I will not sacrifice to the LORD my God burnt offerings that cost me nothing" (24:24). So David paid Araunah 50 shekels of silver, built an altar and sacrificed the oxen. David's sacrifice met with God's favor. God halted the plague and spared the rest of Israel.

(If you are concerned that David's payment—less than $100 in today's silver market—was so paltry for a piece of real estate so obviously valuable, you need to compare the parallel account in First Chronicles 21. There we learn that David paid "six hundred sheckels of gold for the site" [21:25]—something above $70,000 in today's market. How do we explain so gross a discrepancy? Since we believe all Scripture is "God-breathed" and therefore accurate, scholars have conjectured the Second Samuel figure covered just the small threshing floor and Araunah's oxen and implements, while the First Chronicles figure, perhaps negotiated at a later time, included the entire hilltop of approximately four acres on which Solomon later built the temple. Both amounts would satisfy David's insistence to pay "the full price" [1 Chronicles 21:24].)

The unmistakable lesson for us today is that it cost David to save his nation. And it will cost us to save our nation and to obey Christ's command to take His salvation to other nations.

There are four key thoughts in Second Samuel 24:18-25 that apply to our theme of missions by the Book: a *Command*, an *Offering*, a *Sacrifice* and a giving of *Thanks*. I have purposely capitalized the four words. You'll notice that the first letters create the acronym, C-O-S-T, a word from the title of this chapter. The emphasis on cost is deliberate on my part. If there is one thing I want you to remember from this chapter, it is the high cost of missions.

1. A Command

On that day Gad went to David and said to him, "Go up and build an altar to the LORD on the threshing floor of Araunah the Jebusite." So David went up, as the LORD had commanded through Gad. (24:18-19)

Missions Is Not Optional

David was commanded to build an altar that would atone for his sin and the sins of his people. Atonement would bring national salvation from God's wrath. Likewise Jesus has commanded His followers to take the good news of salvation to "all nations"—including our own. Four times in the Bible Jesus' command is reiterated.

For the church at large and for individual believers, the question is not *whether* we will become involved in missions. The question is *how* we will become involved.

It has often been said, "Christ's last command must be our first concern." Many churches and believers have come to regard world missions as one of many equally worthy options from which people may choose. "Let's see," they muse, "we could become involved in camping, day care, radio, missions. Which will it be?" They forget that in Christ's final orders He made it very clear that we are to go into all the world with the gospel; we are to make disciples of all nations. Jesus stated unequivocally that our witness was to begin in our "Jerusalem," but from there it was to extend to the ends of the earth.

How high a priority does your church give to world missions? How involved are you in world missions?

Missions Is Motivated by Worship.

The altar that David was commanded to build was both a place for worship and a place of salvation. First worship, then the saving of Israel. There at the altar David communed with

God. He atoned for his own and his people's sins. His sacrifice stopped the plague and fulfilled his saving mission.

We must always remember that worship, not missions, is our first priority. The first four commandments given by God through Moses to Israel dealt with the people's relationship to God. They were to worship no other gods, they were to make no idols, they were not to misuse the name of the LORD God. They were to honor His day by keeping it holy.

Jesus summed up the Ten Commandments in one succinct statement. " 'Love the Lord your God with all your heart and with all your soul and with all your mind.' This is the first and greatest commandment. And the second is like it: 'Love your neighbor as yourself' " (Matthew 22:37-39).

In His high priestly prayer (John 17), Jesus prayed that His followers would first of all know God and His only Son. Then He prayed for their relationship with each other. Finally He prayed for their mission to the world. That must always be the order of our priorities: God first, then our fellow believers, finally the world. God's worship must always be first and foremost.

"But Tom," you interject. "Aren't you contradicting yourself? You just finished saying Christ's last command is to be our first concern. Now you're insisting that worship of God is to be our first concern."

Let me see if I can reconcile the two statements. It all begins with worship, but true worship will lead us to missions. We haven't truly worshiped if our worship does not motivate us to become involved in world evangelization. True worship and missions are inseparable.

Isaiah serves as a good example. Isaiah the prophet was caught up in a life-changing experience of worship (Isaiah 6). He saw the Lord. He heard the seraphs calling, "Holy, holy, holy," and by contrast he was aware of his own unholiness. But even as Isaiah worshiped, even as he experienced the cleansing of the burning coal, he heard the voice of the Lord asking, "Whom shall I send? And who will go for us?" Then listen to Isaiah's clear-cut commitment to missions: "Here am I. Send me!"

Or consider the Samaritan woman at Jacob's well. She listened to Jesus' classic statement on worship: "God is spirit, and his worshipers must worship in spirit and in truth" (John 4:24). She received the eternally satisfying water of life. Then she hurried off to share this wonderful discovery with her townspeople.

Or read Peter's description of worship: "You also, like living stones, are being built into a spiritual house to be a holy priesthood, offering spiritual sacrifices acceptable to God through Jesus Christ" (1 Peter 2:5). A few verses later, Peter ties such worship inseparably to the evangelistic mandate:

> But you are a chosen people, a royal
> priesthood, a holy nation, a people be-
> longing to God, that you may declare the
> praises of him who called you out of dark-
> ness into his wonderful light (2:9).

Having offered spiritual sacrifices in worship,
we are then to become involved in proclaiming
to others the excellencies of our God. According to Matthew, Jesus' missionary commission
was voiced in the context of worship. "Then
the eleven disciples went to Galilee, to the
mountain where Jesus had told them to go.
When they saw him, they worshiped him. . . .
Then Jesus came to them and said, . . . 'Go and
make disciples of all nations' " (Matthew 28:16-
19).

The root meaning of our English word *worship* is "worth-ship." We sing, "Thou art worthy. . . ." If Jesus really is worthy of our praise
(and He is), we will certainly be motivated to
get up off our knees and out of our sanctuaries
to share His marvelous salvation with those
who know Him not! Jesus' first-century disciples felt that way. They worshiped their resurrected Lord. Shortly thereafter, they were
setting out to tell the good news about Jesus to
the nations of the world.

Missions Begins with the Heart.

David's worship and mission began with an
altar. Altars are prevalent almost anywhere a

person travels. In Vietnam there were ancestral altars in nearly every home. I have seen in Japan altars dedicated to the World War II suicide pilots. In India, a land where it is claimed there are more gods than people, there are elaborate temples and altars everywhere.

Altars are pervasive. But humankind's best altar is not tangible and external. It is within. It is that seat of personality, that inner center of our being—what we have come to refer to as the heart. If our bodies are the temples of the Holy Spirit, our hearts are the altar.

In April, 1952, Donna Stadsklev captured my heart. A long 28 months later, she and I were married. She had captured my body. And it wasn't long until she had my checkbook! Donna exerts tremendous influence over me. I think about her throughout the day. There is nothing I wouldn't do for her.

In a similar way, when Jesus takes His rightful place of rule in our lives, we will want to please Him—even to the point of death.

Have *you* responded to Jesus' command to make disciples of all nations? Is love for Jesus your motivation? Have you made your heart His altar? Does God truly possess you?

2. An Offering

Araunah said to David, "Let my lord the king take whatever pleases him and offer it up. Here are oxen for the burnt offering, and here are threshing sledges and ox yokes for the wood. O king, Araunah gives all this to the king." (24:22-23)

True worship and missions demand our best offerings. In Old Testament times, blemished sheep, lame goats, sick pigeons were unacceptable for God's altar. Only the best of the herd or flock and the firstfruits of the field were fit for offerings. Today, we suppose we can get by with less. Some believers are tempted to offer God the hand-me-downs, the leftovers, the no-longer-useful things. Some people budget for everything from steak to cat food and bird seed. Then if they happen to have some left-over change, they'll put it in the church offering plate.

Araunah gave more than simply an unblemished offering. He gave the best he had. He gave all! The threshing floor was his place of business. His oxen and their yokes were today's equivalent of a farmer's tractor or a businessman's car. The threshing sledges were his tools of trade. What a model Araunah turns out to be! In essence he gave over his whole business to God. He offered it all for divine purposes!

Araunah reminds me of Stanley Tam, the well-known American layman whose book, *God Owns My Business,* has inspired many men. When Tam turned his life over to God, God showed him a way to reclaim silver from photographic developing solution. Stanley Tam turned that business over to God. God gave him another business in plastics that was 10 times as successful. Now Tam has turned that business over to God as well, and he has a worldwide ministry in speaking, broadcasting, writing and witnessing.

At Christ Community Church in Omaha, where I ministered as Pastor of Outreach, I could introduce you to people who have followed Stanley Tam's example. They started with a typewriter, some plumbing tools, a gas station, a heating/air conditioning business. They have turned everything over to God, and He has blessed them. A king—especially the King of kings—deserves all we have.

And that brings me to our third point. Worship and missions also involve . . .

3. A Sacrifice

"O king, Araunah gives all this to the king." Araunah also said to him, "May the LORD your God accept you."

But the king replied to Araunah, "No, I insist on paying you for it. I will not sacrifice to the LORD my God burnt offerings that cost me nothing. (24:23-24)

True Worship and Missions Cost
Eternal life may be a free gift, but worship, if it is from the heart, costs something! David did not expect it to be otherwise.

As I mentioned earlier, Araunah's threshing floor that David purchased was a significant spot. David would be building an altar and presenting his burnt offering to God on the site where Abraham offered Isaac his son. Only a few years later, it would be the site of Solomon's temple with its brazen altar of sacrifice. How significant David's sacrifice! What an example for us today as we consider the cost of missions!

At least in America, when we give someone a gift, we make sure the price tag has been removed first! When we put money in the offering plate at church, we hope the people around us won't know the denomination of the bill or the amount of our check. If we pledge money for missions or the building fund, we want to be assured that our name will not be identified with the sum.

But there is One for whom the amount of our gift is no secret. Christ saw the widow's mite. He knew the cost of the perfume with which Mary anointed Him. And He is aware of what we give to Him.

In my missionary service in Vietnam I've encountered sacrifice perhaps more often than in America. I can recall yet, though it was 30 years ago, an elderly woman, too poor for bus fare, who walked a considerable distance over a mountain pass in order to attend church. She carried a chicken and some eggs as her offering to the Lord. They were all she had, but she counted it a privilege to give to God. Sacrifice!

Another Vietnamese worship experience is deeply engraved on my heart. I had walked across hot sand to reach the village of Xuan-Loc, where I was to preach at a new church. The building was very modest: bamboo slats part way up for walls, thatched roof, makeshift benches, no floor except the sand. A little red-colored cross identified the structure as a church.

When I arrived, several new believers were already there to welcome me. Amid their cheery greetings I suddenly heard a voice from—of all places—the ground! The sound startled me. As I looked down, I saw a severely handicapped man. He had no crutches, no wheelchair, no car. On his hands and knees he had *crawled* more than a mile, across that scorching sand, in order to worship with us. Sacrifice!

True Worship and Missions Will Touch Our Pocketbooks.

David "paid fifty shekels of silver" (24:24) for Araunah's threshing floor and oxen. David was not willing to take the ground and the animals as a gift. He refused to offer to God what cost him nothing.

God prompted His prophet Malachi to tell the Israelites they were robbing God. "Will a man rob God?" He asks through Malachi. "Yet you rob me" (Malachi 3:8). God goes on to explain:

But you ask, "How do we rob you?"
"In tithes and offerings. You are under a curse—the whole nation of you—because you are robbing me. Bring the whole tithe into the storehouse, that there may be food in my house." (Malachi 3:8-10)

The tithe—10 percent of our income—is the bare minimum that we should be bringing to the Lord. And if you wish to argue that the tithe is legalistic, I will counter that it far predates the law. Abraham gave Melchizedek, king of Salem and "priest of God Most High, . . . a tenth of everything" (Genesis 14:18-20). Moses and the law would not come for another 600 years. And if you are applying New Testament grace to giving, Christ came to fulfill the law and to take us beyond the law!

In 1989 I took a team from Christ Community Church in Omaha to Nigeria for an Evangelism Explosion leadership clinic. On Sunday of our week in Nigeria, our team worshiped with our Nigerian brothers and sisters. It was another unforgettable experience in sacrificial giving. In fact, for me the high point of the morning service was the offering. I should explain that the church was located in what used to be called Biafra. It was in the region where so much starvation had occurred some years earlier. Yet those Christians, and I mean all of them, filed to the front of their church in a dance offering to the Lord. Their faces were aglow as they put their tithes in a big box marked "Tithes" and their offerings above and beyond the tithe on a large platter. As they gave, they sang to the beat of drums and tambourines:

> *We will not serve mammon;*
> *We will serve the Lord.*
> *We are satisfied in Jesus;*
> *He our every need supplies.*

If ever I witnessed cheerful, sacrificial giving, that was the time and the place!

4. A Giving of Thanks

To be truly biblical, worship and missions must culminate in thanksgiving to God. We read that on the threshing floor he had bought from Araunah David "sacrificed burnt offerings and fellowship offerings" (24:25).

Fellowship offerings were thank offerings to God for all His mercies. The burnt offerings brought God's forgiveness to David and his people. The burnt offerings saved David and Israel from God's further judgment. How appropriate, therefore, that David should also offer thank offerings to God.

True Worship and Missionary Giving Issue from Grateful Hearts

I have no desire to send you on a guilt trip. I want you to go on a *gratitude journey* the rest of your life! Are you grateful for your salvation? How grateful? Are you grateful enough to give God a generous and sacrificial thank offering?

Paul said to the Romans: "I urge you, brothers, in view of God's mercy, to offer your bodies as living sacrifices, holy and pleasing to God—this is your spiritual act of worship" (Romans 12:1). Out of gratitude for God's mercies we give Him our hearts, our bodies, our money. We give Him *everything!* And when we give Him everything, we discover that . . .

True Worship and Missionary Giving Move the Heart of God

I like the way the New American Standard Bible concludes the report of David's sacrifice on Araunah's threshing floor: "Thus the LORD was moved by entreaty for the land, and the plague was held back from Israel" (24:25). Did you realize that when you give God costly offerings you move Him deeply? You give Him great delight. You bless His heart. His work advances. The church is built up. God's kingdom expands into new frontiers. His servants' needs are supplied. His will is done.

But there is one more benefit.

True Sacrifice Moves the Hand of God

The hand of God that brought the plague now held it back from destroying Israel as a nation. When God's heart is touched, His hands reach out on behalf of His people. God's hand is a loving hand, a generous hand, a rewarding hand.

When God told Israel through Malachi to "bring the whole tithe into the storehouse," He promised a blessing for obedience. " 'Test me in this,' says the LORD Almighty, 'and see if I will not throw open the floodgates of heaven and pour out so much blessing that you will not have room enough for it' " (Malachi 3:10). If that isn't moving the hand of God, I don't know what is! God seems to be saying, "I'm never going to let you outgive Me. If you'll sacrificially give to Me and to My work, I'll bless you beyond measure! I'll bless you so much you won't be able to deny it!"

Were you aware that some preachers hesitate to say anything about money and giving? They're afraid of offending people. Or they're afraid people will think they're begging just to "feather their own nest." I must confess that I *love* to speak about money. Do you know why? Because I know that God returns so much blessing to those who give to Him!

But let me clarify one thing. We are not to give to God so that God will bless us. We are to give because God has blessed us. We are to give out of gratitude and love. We are to give out of obedience to His Word and as an expression of our worship. But when we give from those motives, God is not going to let us outgive Him.

Nyack College, where I studied, had—and has—an annual missionary conference. As a freshman, and motivated by those who spoke to us that week, I pledged $25 for missions. I was working eight hours a night three nights a week to put myself through school. Every dollar I earned was important and very carefully spent. A $25 pledge does not seem like much today, but it was a lot back then!

Did I give so God would bless me? No, I gave out of my love for God and His work. Did He bless me? Yes, indeed! The following summer God gave me a good source of income. In my sophomore year, He helped me find a daytime job that adequately met my needs. So that year I doubled my missionary pledge to $50. Each week I was able to put a dollar in the offering plate for missions, meeting the pledged amount in full. That summer I delivered Dr. Pepper soft drinks in Burlington, Iowa, as I related earlier, earning enough to cover my tuition. Again I doubled my missionary pledge—not so God would bless me but because He already had blessed me.

That next summer, Donna and I were married, and we got the job of managing the college store. Again, we doubled our missions pledge—to $200.

The next year, to our great surprise, our church's missions division asked us to leave for Vietnam without the usual two years of home service. Arriving overseas, we began to tithe our missionary allowance, a practice we continued for over 20 years. And God's blessing was always evident.

While pastoring in Hong Kong after Vietnam closed to us, I read a sermon by Dr. D. James Kennedy on the subject of giving. He told how he felt led of God to increase his giving from one tithe to two, then three, then four, until finally he gave his entire pastor's salary back to the church! I was impressed. I was also incredulous. How could the man survive?

Then Archie Parrish, one of Kennedy's associate pastors, visited Hong Kong, and I asked him to confirm Kennedy's testimony. Archie replied that not only was what Dr. Kennedy said true, but it had impacted Kennedy's staff to increase their giving.

I broached the subject with my wife while we were on vacation. "Donna, could you stretch your faith and sacrifice with me to *double* our tithe?" We were still on missionary allowance—not a large sum when it came to meeting living expenses. But after much prayer and heart-searching, we decided to do it.

I must confess, that first month was not easy. God, however, began to bless. The apartment where we were living was in the noisiest part of a noisy city. The church board found us a much quieter, more pleasant apartment only a block from the church.

Then a letter arrived from our church headquarters. My mother's college roommate had died, leaving her estate to the work of eight missionaries. I was one of the eight. I stood to receive $26,000 for my ministry! The very morning that letter arrived, I had been at a missionary prayer meeting praying with others that God would supply funds to move a rooftop chapel to a new location. Immediately I telephoned our field director to say that God had answered our prayers!

There was enough money left over for me to replace our dilapidated old Volkswagon with a new Honda Civic. When I saw the license plate, I almost laughed out loud. The numbers were preceded by the two letters "BT." I said to Donna, "They stand for the Blessing of the Tithe! In fact, a *double* blessing for the *double* tithe!"

True worship is costly. But it moves the heart and the hand of God! He is committed to bless generous givers. And because He is also a giving God, He will not let anyone outgive Him.

Have you received the free gift of eternal life? If so, how grateful are you for the sacrifice that purchased that gift? Have you expressed that gratitude to God?

Don't ever forget it. Eternal life is free, but true worship is costly!

Study Guide Questions

1. If eternal life is free, why do churches ask for offerings?

2. How would you answer a Christian who says, "Missions is optional"?

3. From a Bible viewpoint, how are worship and missions related?

4. "Worship and missions, if they are truly from the heart, are costly." Do you agree or disagree with the statement? Why?

5. What is the difference between giving out of guilt and giving out of gratitude?

6. Second Samuel 24:25 informs us that "the LORD answered [David's] prayer in behalf of the land, and the plague on Israel was stopped." According to 24:24-25, what actions of David may have moved God to answer his prayer?

7. What must be our true motive for giving to God and to His work of world evangelization?

8. Why do you suppose God blesses those who with proper motives give to Him and His work?

Chapter Eleven

Our Mission of Mercy

Matthew 9

W HAT WE WERE AS CHILDREN WE ARE as adults. That observation has been expressed in various terms, but it is an almost universally accepted principle. The Roman Catholic Church says, "Give us a child until he is seven and he will be a Catholic for life." The Bible says, "Train a child in the way he should go, / and when he is old he will not turn from it" (Proverbs 22:6).

When it comes to mercy, the instruction and the example cannot begin too soon. I had the great good fortune to be reared in a home full of mercy. If anyone ever had the gift of mercy, it was my missionary mother—Mary Hartman Stebbins. From sunup to sundown she ministered to people in need. Was the supplicant hungry? She managed to find him food. Penniless? She dug into her purse. Cold? She looked through the closet for a coat or sweater. In need of help with studies? She seemed to have endless time for tutoring. Mother was a model of Christian mercy. Her example made a profound impression on me.

Perhaps that is why Matthew 5:7 became one of my favorite Bible verses: "Blessed are the merciful, / for they will be shown mercy." The brief couplet, so succinct, so truthful, has been engraved deeply on my heart, my mind and my experience. I have sought to apply the principle to my life and ministry, both overseas and here in North America.

But what exactly do we refer to when we speak of "mercy"? At Bible college I heard mercy defined as God's withholding from us the wrath we so justly deserve. The definition, albeit true, provides us only one aspect of mercy. It is a rather negative, passive aspect at that.

Robert Thune, senior pastor at Christ Community Church in Omaha, added another dimension to my understanding. "Mercy," Pastor Thune said, "understands misery and reaches out to help." I like that! Mercy identifies with those who suffer. It empathizes with them. But it doesn't stop there. It reaches out a helping hand in loving, thoughtful, appropriate ways. It matches loving words with compassionate deeds.

Jesus, the epitome of mercy, expresses both of these aspects in His earthly life and ministry.

Because of Jesus' redemptive death, we who believe are spared the divine wrath we so justly deserve. Because Jesus took on our human nature, He understands the misery we endure and reaches out to us a helping, healing hand.

John the Baptist, in the depression of his imprisonment, sent some of his disciples to make sure Jesus was the promised Messiah. How did Jesus respond?

"Go back and report to John what you hear and see: The blind receive sight, the lame walk, those who have leprosy are cured, the deaf hear, the dead are raised, and the good news is preached to the poor" (Matthew 11:4-5). Wherever Jesus went He identified with those in misery. In mercy He reached out to help them.

Missionary work, if it is to be truly effective, must include expressions of Christian mercy. That is the thesis of this chapter. I invite you to examine with me a mercy-packed day in the life of Jesus. We find the details in Matthew 9. We will be noting four aspects of Jesus' mission of mercy: *His dual approach, His desire, His demonstration* and *His delegation of responsibility to others.* We turn first to . . .

1. Jesus' Dual Approach to Mercy

Jesus stepped into a boat, crossed over and came to his own town. Some men brought to him a paralytic, lying on a mat. When Jesus saw their faith, he said to the paralytic, "Take heart, son; your sins are forgiven." (9:1-2)

Notice that Jesus was primarily concerned about the paralyzed man's spiritual condition. He addressed first the man's sins and assured him, as only Jesus could, that his sins were forgiven. Likewise the missionary's primary ministry is to bring to lost, sinful people the saving good news of Jesus Christ. We do not cross oceans and cultures simply as agents of social services. We don't learn languages, adjust to foreign customs, brave disease and danger just to minister to people's bodies and minds.

The American church is increasingly aware of the disparity between living conditions here and those of most other lands. Some missionaries, particularly those serving with more liberal churches, have shifted their focus. Instead of concern for people's eternal destiny, their chief concern is how to improve people's living conditions now. Christ's missionary mandate has been eclipsed by temporal concerns.

The root cause of humankind's suffering is sin. It has been that way ever since Adam and Eve's disobedience and God's judgment on them. A missionary message that does not address the problem of sin is like aspirin for appendicitis.

On the other hand, Jesus, the Creator God, was well aware of the human psyche. He knew that people are need-oriented. It is hard to think of much else when one is terribly hungry. Or racked with pain. Or about to be put out on the street. It's hard to concentrate on eternal salvation when temporal needs are so insistent, so demanding. Jesus knew that. And so we have what I call His dual approach to mercy:

> "So that you may know that the Son of Man has authority on earth to forgive sins. . . ." Then he said to the paralytic, "Get up, take your mat and go home." (9:6)

Following Jesus' example, biblically-oriented missionaries have continued to lead the way in medicine, education, relief and social services—but always with an unmistakable emphasis on evangelism and the eternal destiny of the people they help. This dual thrust has led to the salvation of millions of people and the establishment of churches on every continent. Missions done by the Book takes this dual approach. But in keeping with the New Testament pattern, the priority is on evangelism and church planting.

During our second term of missionary service in Vietnam, Donna and I worked in the royal city of Hue, my birthplace. Buddhism and ancestor worship were firmly entrenched in Hue. The citizens were proud of their historic association with Vietnam's royalty. We found people to be self-satisfied and very resistant to the gospel. How could we get through to them? Did they have any felt needs that we could meet?

It suddenly occurred to us that the families of Hue had sons who were dying on the battle-fields. That was the case throughout South Vietnam. Many of the young men were returning with critical wounds or excruciatingly painful burns. Others had lost legs or arms. Like the paralytic in Matthew 9, they needed help.

In Saigon, World Vision had developed a wonderful mission of mercy. Through gifts of compassionate people in America, they provided crutches and wheelchairs to wounded Vietnamese soldiers. They also made up packets of towels, soap and other amenities. Some of our own missionaries were going bed-to-bed at Cong Hoa Military Hospital, distributing these things. For those who were ambulatory, they held a gospel service every Sunday evening in the hospital's large auditorium. Christian films, music, testimonies and evangelistic messages presented Christ's saving truth: "Take heart, son; your sins are forgiven."

We saw the great value of this dual approach. So we asked World Vision if we could help them in a similar ministry at Hue Military Hospital. What a marvelous mission of mercy emerged!

One of the first wounded soldiers we met at the hospital was a young sergeant. He had been returning from leave—married just three days—when the bus he was riding hit an enemy mine. Both his legs had to be amputated. Now he and his new wife faced a very hard, different life. But not without hope. Through the generosity of Christians in America I was able to give him a wheelchair that would provide mobility.

Scores of such young men found physical help in their time of tremendous need. Then, as we presented them with gospel tracts and held evangelistic meetings, many of them put their trust in Christ our Savior.

Thank God for Jesus' model of a dual approach to humankind's physical and spiritual needs!

2. Jesus' Desire for Mercy

As Jesus went on from there, he saw a man named Matthew sitting at the tax collector's booth. "Follow me," he told him, and Matthew got up and followed him.

While Jesus was having dinner at Matthew's house, many tax collectors and "sinners" came and ate with him and his disciples. When the Pharisees saw this, they asked his disciples, "Why does your teacher eat with tax collectors and 'sinners'?"

On hearing this, Jesus said, "It is not the healthy who need a doctor, but the sick.

But go and learn what this means: 'I desire mercy, not sacrifice.' For I have not come to call the righteous, but sinners." (9:9-13)

Here Jesus sets forth His philosophy of ministry. It wasn't sacrifice—the typical Jewish expression of ceremonial worship with oxen, lambs, goats and turtledoves. Rather, it was mercy. It was understanding people in their need and reaching out to help them. Jesus could have been in the temple with the religious people of His day offering sacrifices. Instead, He was in the home of a tax collector on a ministry of mercy. Mercy was what Jesus desired most!

Notice also Jesus' use of the analogy of medicine. "It is not the healthy who need a doctor, but the sick." Matthew, a sinner, needed Jesus. That's why Jesus was there.

This medicine metaphor calls to my mind another ministry of mercy in Vietnam that proved extremely fruitful. Both at Banmethuot and at Pleiku, our missionaries saw the importance of developing a ministry to leprous people. Early on in both places leprosy clinics were an important part of the missionaries' ministries. At Banmethuot, they developed deep in the jungle a complete hospital primarily for leprosy patients. Our third child was born in that hospital. Over the month that Donna and I were there, I had a good opportunity to see the dual ministry of the care providers. Dr. Ardel Vietti and her staff of missionary nurses—Millie Ade, Dawn Deets, Olive Kingsbury, Ruth Wilting—had a most effective ministry. Not only did they work to relieve the physical suffering of those with leprosy, but scores of the patients at the leprosarium found Christ as Savior. And not only the patients. Family members and friends accompanied the patients, and they saw the love of Christ demonstrated in unmistakable terms. Reports of this ministry of mercy and love spread far and wide among the villages of the highlands. People were convinced that Christianity must be the only true way to God.

Later, a leprosarium was completed at Pleiku, as well. I will never forget the response of one of the Vietnamese patients at Pleiku when I asked him how he liked it at the hospital.

"Thank the Lord, everything is well!" he exclaimed. I asked him where he was from, and he told me he had grown up in North Vietnam. As a teen, he had received Christ and was active in a church youth group. His father, however, forbade him to follow "the way of Christ." Without Christian teaching, he renounced his faith and became a communist.

Not long after that, his father died. An elder brother was killed for the sole reason that he was a landowner. The young man fled into Laos and finally crossed over into South Vietnam. Then, to his shock, he discovered that he had somehow contracted leprosy. He tried every imaginable cure, but the disease progressed, slowly but inexorably. He watched his fingers stiffen and slowly disappear. Desperate and hopeless, he wondered about his fate.

One day he heard of a leprosy treatment center in Pleiku. Traveling south, he eventually arrived at the hospital. There he was received graciously and given treatment immediately. It was shortly after that when I met him.

Enthusiastically he expressed appreciation for the missionary nurses and staff who were caring for him. "These people are good to me. This is a very fine place." When I inquired about his spiritual condition he told me of his earlier experiences and let me know he now wanted to return to Christ. We prayed together—a repentant wanderer confessing his sins and entreating Christ to forgive him. Praise followed as he thanked God for His goodness and grace.

I left the hospital on that wind swept hill in Pleiku thanking God that His prodigal son from North Vietnam had returned "home," there to find forgiveness and restoration. And I thanked God for those who worked long hours under incredibly hard circumstances to express the mercy and love of Christ. Their compassion had melted a heart hardened by years of communist influence. Their mission of mercy had paved the way for my message of forgiveness and hope.

That brings us quite naturally to the third aspect of Jesus' mission of mercy. We are calling it . . .

3. Jesus' Demonstration of Mercy

Glance through Matthew 9:18-33 and you will discover a series of Jesus' compassionate miracles. He raised a dead girl to life (9:18-19, 23-26). A simple touch of His cloak brought instant healing to a woman "who had been subject to bleeding for twelve years" (9:20). Jesus mercifully restored sight to two blind men who cried out for mercy (9:27-31). Jesus drove the demon from a mute, and the man spoke (9:32-33). This last act of mercy so amazed the crowd that they cried out: "Nothing like this has ever been seen in Israel." What a demonstration of mercy and love!

People aren't satisfied with hearing a message. They want to see mercy and love in action. Jesus was the perfect incarnation of mercy, the best demonstration of love anyone could ask for! Hurting, hopeless people need someone who cares, someone who will reach out to them in their misery, someone to offer a loving, caring hand.

After my dramatic, 11th-hour departure from Vietnam by helicopter, I received instructions from our mission to proceed to Guam. Guam is a small American island in the mid-Pacific. Already shiploads of Vietnamese refugees were landing on Guam.

Within minutes of my arrival on Guam, I joined several of my missionary colleagues as we met the ships and planes. We served as interpreters for the refugees and gave directions to those needing extra help. If ever I had an opportunity to demonstrate Christ's mercy, that was it!

Very late one night I was on dock duty as a shipload of refugees disembarked. A young Vietnamese woman made her way down the gangplank. In her arms was an Amerasian boy, probably about five years old. As she reached where I was standing, she dumped the little guy in my arms.

"His mother told me to give him to the very first American I met. So he's yours!"

Before I could ask her for any details, the woman disappeared into the crowd. There I stood holding a sleepy, little, motherless, fatherless child in my arms.

I asked him how old he was, and he held up five fingers. I asked him his name, and he answered "Thang!" In Vietnamese the word means "victory"—quite a name considering the defeat both his mother and father had just suffered. Out of what seemed like nowhere, a precious little life had been entrusted to me. What should I do?

I remembered the words of James: "Religion that God our Father accepts as pure and faultless is this: to look after orphans . . . in their distress" (James 1:27).

I hunted down Donna, who was helping other refugees further down the dock. "Here, Honey," I announced, "you have a new son! His name is Thang and he's five years old!"

The hour was too late to ask any of the authorities what to do with Thang. Donna and I decided we should take him home for the rest of the night. Back at our living quarters, Donna tried to peel off Thang's salt-encrusted clothes. They obviously had not been changed for at least 10 days at sea. But every time she started to unbutton his shirt, the little rascal bit her hand. He wasn't about to let a strange white women undress him! So Donna had no choice but to put him in the tub, clothes and all.

When Thang was scrubbed up, we discovered we had a beautiful blonde, curly-headed Vietnamese boy! But what were we going to do with him? God had put him in our care for a purpose. But what was it?

Then Donna and I remembered a Christian helicopter pilot whom we had come to know in Danang. Donna had been able to find a Vietnamese orphan baby girl for Bob and Rhoda Atcheson to adopt. They had begged us to look for another child. But would they take a five-year-old Amerasian?

By then it was around 4 in the morning on Guam. Back in Orlando, Florida, however, where Bob and Rhoda lived, it was still daytime. We decided to telephone them to see if they were interested. Bob never hesitated.

"Sure, we'll take the little guy!" he shouted.

"But there's an important condition," I added. "I don't know if you'll be willing, but it's the only way I can get Thang to you. You'll have to sponsor a Vietnamese pastor and his family of seven children. Then they can bring Thang to you as one of their children."

This time, Bob's response was not quite as quick. That would be a lot of mouths to fill and a lot of beds to find. But he and Rhoda agreed.

Later that morning we returned to the base with Thang and looked up the tent where Pastor Nguyen hoai Duc and his family were housed. Could he handle one more child? Would he be willing to take Thang to America? Would he settle in Orlando, Florida, and plant a Vietnamese church there?

To our delight, the Ducs agreed. And in a few days we saw our little blond-headed orphan boy off to mainland America.

The Atchesons renamed Thang *Thomas*—after the missionary who found him in the wee hours of the morning on the docks of Guam! What a suitable home God has given him! His older brother Bob is pure American. His younger sister Heather is pure Vietnamese. And Tom, in the middle, is half American, half Vietnamese! More importantly, they are all members of a strong evangelical church. Today the children all know Christ as their Savior. Tom plays the trumpet, graduated from high school with straight A's and presently is attending a good college.

4. Jesus' Delegation
of Responsibility to Others

There is one more aspect of Christ's mission of mercy in Matthew 9. Jesus enlisted others who would have a share in His ministry.

> When [Jesus] saw the crowds, he had compassion on them, because they were harassed and helpless, like sheep without a shepherd. Then he said to his disciples, "The harvest is plentiful but the workers are few. Ask the Lord of the harvest, therefore, to send out workers into his harvest field." (9:36-38)

What a lesson in mercy from the Master! Mercy for the physical part of the person as well as the spiritual part. Mercy above the externals of religious rote. Mercy demonstrated in tangible acts. Now, Jesus' delegation of this ministry of mercy to His followers.

Three thoughts stand out: (1) Christ's own ministry continued to be dual—to the whole person; (2) The objects of Jesus' mercy became the agents of His mercy; (3) As Jesus encountered increased numbers who needed mercy, He multiplied the dispensers of mercy.

Christ expected those who had received His mercy to extend it to others. He said, "Freely you have received, freely give" (Matthew 10:8). And again, "As the Father has sent me, I am sending you" (John 20:21). His followers, moreover, obeyed His command and fulfilled His desire. Having been objects of His mercy, they became instruments of that mercy.

Hence we find Peter and John mercifully reaching out to a lame man at the temple gate, extending to him Christ's healing (Acts 3:1-8). We find "Stephen, a man full of God's grace and power, [doing] great wonders and miraculous signs among the people" (Acts 6:8). Later he prays for God's mercy upon those who were in the very act of stoning him to death (Acts 7:60)! We see Philip mercifully bring healing, deliverance from unclean spirits and the good news of eternal life to the people of Samaria (Acts 8:4-8). We see faithful Ananias going to Saul, the leading persecutor of the church. Ananias prayed for Saul that he might receive his sight and be filled with the Holy Spirit (Acts 9:10-19).

We see Tabitha (Dorcas), a widow in Joppa, "always doing good and helping the poor" (Acts 9:36). We witness Paul in Lystra as he reaches out in mercy to a crippled man who had never walked. To that man Paul extends God's healing grace (Acts 14:8-10). We watch Paul and Silas in the dungeon at Philippi, backs raw from the beatings dealt them by the magistrates. What do they do? They show mercy to their jailer, bringing the gift of eternal life to him and his whole household (Acts 16:22-34).

Christ desires the same of us today. He, the Head of the church, delegates to us, its members, a mission of mercy. We are to be His instruments of mercy in the midst of our hurting, sinning, dying society. Christ longs to meet needs, administer healing, bring forgiveness and share His eternal life—through us.

As Jesus "went through all the towns and villages, teaching, . . . preaching, . . . healing" (Matthew 9:35), excitement seemed to mount. The crowds were so massive that Matthew describes them as "sheep without a shepherd" (9:36). The scene reminds me of the Vietnamese "boat people" Donna and I encountered in Hong Kong.

After a year on Guam, I agreed to be pastor of Kowloon Tong Church's English-speaking congregation. We had been there but a short time before the boat people began arriving by the hundreds. Even without these new refugees, Hong Kong was a crowded city. When the Vietnamese began arriving, I went down to the docks on my day off to assist them in any way I could.

The crush of humanity was almost unbelievable. They were crowded into uninsulated steel warehouses. Families of eight to 10 members had to take turns lying on a mat the size of a double bed. They stood on the docks in long lines, little tin can in hand, waiting their turn at the water faucet. If they moved too fast on the docks, they risked bumping someone into the bay. That's how crowded things were. My heart almost broke as I surveyed the scene. I think I experienced a little of the compassion Christ must have felt as He saw the crowds "harassed and helpless, like sheep without a shepherd."

One of the refugees in that mass of humanity was Trieu van An. In 1954, when Trieu was but two years old, his mother and his Chinese father boarded a southbound refugee ship to escape the communist control of North Vietnam. The family settled in Saigon, where Trieu's father opened a dry goods shop.

Trieu attended school in Saigon, worked in his father's shop and eventually secured a position stocking shelves at a U.S. Army Post Exchange. That is what he was doing when Saigon fell to the North Vietnamese in April, 1975.

Following the communist takeover, Trieu was without a job, and the communists assigned him to stoke the blast furnace of a nearby steel mill. About that time, also, Trieu met a soft-spoken young South Vietnamese girl, Phuong, and soon fell in love. Trieu faithfully saved his meager earnings for the dowry that would enable him to marry Phuong.

It took nearly three years, but at last he had the required price. Before he could present the money to his future father-in-law, however, communist cadres got wind of Trieu's hoard. Bursting into his home, they confiscated the entire dowry.

For Trieu, it was the last straw. For three years he had endured numerous injustices at the hands of the new government. He had watched conditions deteriorate in South Vietnam. When he learned of a group who planned to escape, he signed on. So did Phuong and her parents.

They were promised a boat well stocked with food and water and manned by experienced sailors. Passengers would number not more than 200. Instead, as they covertly boarded the 60-foot fishing junk, they found double that number of passengers. There was barely standing room. Elderly couples, pregnant women and 10 newborn babies jostled each other for space.

By the fourth tumultuous day at sea, the bungling sailors had managed to cover only 100 miles. Supplies of food and water were exhausted. The boat leaked badly. The rudder had broken. Ten-foot waves threatened to swallow the boatful of panic-stricken refugees.

"Until that desperate moment," Trieu recalled, "I had never found any time for God. I was always too busy to think about spiritual matters. But as death approached, I suddenly awakened. I saw how very small I was and how immense was the sea and vast the sky. For the first time my attention turned to the greatness of God. I realized that He alone could rescue me from such a hopeless plight. I cried to Him for mercy."

God's answer was timely. About noon, they saw a ship on the horizon. Ecstatic, the refugees waved and shouted frantically. More practically, they raised a makeshift SOS flag, hoping to attract the ship's attention.

The *S.S. Whipple,* a U.S. Navy frigate on a routine trip from Bangkok to Hong Kong, spotted the flag and pulled alongside the failing junk. For two hours, American sailors risked their lives in a precarious rescue operation. Dangling from safety lines, they caught the children thrown to them, passing their human burdens over their shoulders to other men above. As adults on the stricken craft clambered into lifeboats, the lightened junk rocked more fiercely in the heavy seas, sending other passengers sprawling into the water.

Phuong's father scrambled up a rope ladder, but then at the last moment slipped and plunged into the sea, landing between the ship and the junk. Seconds before he would have been crushed between the vessels, he grabbed a lifeline and was hauled aboard the navy ship. Shortly after the last two refugees were whisked to safety, the ill-fated fishing craft sank.

The *Whipple* proceeded full speed to Hong Kong, where Trieu and the rest of the grateful refugees were given a warm reception and permission to remain for three months. Two hundred of the new refugees, including Trieu, Phuong and her family, were tucked away in a vacant Chinese villa just five blocks from Kowloon Tong Church that I pastored. With his command of Vietnamese, Chinese and English, Trieu was appointed as one of the three people responsible for order in the makeshift "camp."

He was on duty the evening a few weeks later when our team of Vietnamese-speaking pastors and missionaries visited the camp to distribute used clothing and gospel literature and to show a Vietnamese Christian film. Trieu welcomed us enthusiastically and sat in rapt attention during the evangelistic message that followed. At the close, he and his future father-in-law were among seven men and women who responded to the invitation to receive Christ.

"It wasn't difficult to understand or believe," Trieu reflected later. "I had seen the hand of God save me on three previous occasions: once from the North Vietnamese, again from the communists in the South and then from certain death at sea."

Several weeks later, Phuong also turned to Christ at a similar meeting. And not long after that I had the joy of uniting the happy couple in marriage at our nearby church.

Your memories may be far less suspenseful than those of Trieu and Phuong (who now live in Hatfield, Pennsylvania). But certainly God's mercy is just as unmistakable. As a recipient of His mercy, you in turn are to be an agent of that mercy to others. Remember what Jesus said in His Sermon on the Mount:

> Blessed are the merciful,
>   for they will be shown mercy.
>   (Matthew 5:7)

Study Guide Questions

1. How would you define the word *mercy*?

2. What two facets of mercy are suggested in the chapter you have just read?

3. What was Jesus' uppermost concern for the paralytic? What should be the missionary's primary focus?

4. Why do you think Jesus so zealously and compassionately reached out to meet people's felt needs?

5. Why today do you think it is imperative that missionaries demonstrate Christ's love through acts of mercy?

6. What are some of the compassionate ways missionaries today are reaching out to needy people?

7. What are possible ways you or your church might express Christ's mercy to hurting, needy people in your community?

Chapter Twelve

Clay Pots

Second Corinthians 4

JIM ELLIOT, MARTYRED MISSIONARY TO the Auca Indians of Ecuador, once called missionaries "a bunch of nobodies trying to exalt Somebody."[1] His words remind us of a first-century missionary—Paul—who referred to himself and his team members as clay pots bearing invaluable treasure (2 Corinthians 4:7).

God chooses and uses some very ordinary people to proclaim His gospel to the ends of the earth. I know, because I am one of them! God takes this approach in order to display His power and magnify His glory. As an overseas missionary for 25 years and later a homeland pastor, I can only marvel.

Christ began the whole missionary movement with a handful of very ordinary people: converted fishermen, tax collectors and tent-makers. In his earlier letter to the Corinthians Paul said:

Brothers, think of what you were when you were called. Not many of you were wise by human standards; not many were influential; not many were of noble birth. But God chose the foolish things of the world to shame the wise; God chose the weak things of the world to shame the strong. He chose the lowly things of this world and the despised things—and the things that are not—to nullify the things that are, so that no one may boast before him. (1 Corinthians 1:26-29)

Then he adds in Second Corinthians 4:7: "We have this treasure in jars of clay to show that this all-surpassing power is from God and not from us." In a handful of well-chosen, graphic words, Paul describes the missionary.

"Just how," you ask, "do missionaries resemble clay pots?" I suggest three similarities.

First, we are unattractive and fragile—just as *clay* is. Every time I look in the mirror, every time I take inventory of my personal strengths or gifts, I marvel that God chose this less-than-attractive, fragile person as one of His missionaries!

Second, we missionaries are a very *common* lot. In and of ourselves in that foreign setting, we are of no great value. We are just ordinary people undistinguished except for our foreignness.

Third, our real value lies in what we *contain.* Our calling and commission is to carry Christ and His gospel to lost people. Whom we take, not what we amount to, is the critical point.

Perhaps you are asking, "How, then, could Paul and how can missionaries today benefit the cause of Christ? How can they advance His gospel?" The answer is spelled out in Second Corinthians 4. To be used of God, missionaries must (1) carry *precious treasure from God* (2) in the *power of God*. They must (3) yield to *painful processing by God,* and (4) evidence *progress and fruitfulness in God*. Their motive must be (5) *praise and glory to God*.

1. Missionaries Must Carry Precious Treasure from God

What is the "treasure" we "clay pot" missionaries contain and carry? If you'll take another look at the word *treasure* in our text, you'll notice that it is preceded by the demonstrative pronoun *this*. The apostle is evidently pointing back to earlier verses that specify what the treasure is. Let's see if we can discover exactly what Paul means when he speaks of "treasure."

In 4:2 Paul says he does not "distort the word of God" but rather "set[s] forth the truth plainly." In 4:3, he speaks of "our gospel" being veiled from some people. In 4:4, he says the minds of unbelievers have been blinded by the god of this age to prevent them from seeing "the light of the gospel of the glory of Christ." In 4:5 Paul declares that he and his associates preach "Jesus Christ as Lord." In 4:6 he declares that God shone "the light of the knowledge of the glory of God in the face of Christ" into his heart.

This which Paul calls "truth" (4:2), "our gospel (good news)" (4:3), "the light" (4:4) is in reality a Person, "Jesus Christ" (4:5). As Paul says to the Romans, "The gospel is centered in God's Son" (Romans 1:3, Phillips). What a wonderful message we missionaries have to communicate! What a great responsibility and privilege we have!

My wife's parents were pioneer missionaries to Côte d'Ivoire, West Africa. At one point in their ministry they had established a new base and were working desperately to complete a permanent building there before the rainy season set in. A woman arrived from a distant village.

"I am told you are a man of God," she said to Dad Stadsklev. "Would you come to my village? We've been waiting many years for you!"

Dad Stadsklev explained that he was in the midst of completing a needed building. "I promise to visit your village as soon as I have finished this building," he assured the woman.

"All right," she answered with resignation. "I will wait for you." The woman was prepared to wait—right there—until the project was completed! In Ivorian culture, her lodging and food would be the Stadsklev's responsibility. They had neither space nor extra food for such an obligation.

"No, go back to your village," my father-in-law countered. "I will come very soon."

"But I cannot return without you," the woman insisted. "The others will not forgive me if, after finding you, I fail to bring you to them."

Dad had no alternative but to arrange with an Ivorian deacon to take over his building duties while he and a Baouli pastor accompanied the woman 30 miles to her village. There the two men were escorted to the hut of an elderly villager obviously nearing the end of life.

"You've come at last!" the old man exclaimed. "Where have you been these years? Many years ago we sent a young man south to pay our head tax. There he heard a wonderful story and became a Christian. He was told to return to his village, burn his fetishes and build a 'house of God.' He was told a white man would come to tell all our villagers more of God's Word."

The elderly man continued. "So we burned our fetishes, built a 'house of God' and waited for the white man. But no white man came. The house of God grew old and fell down. We built another, and another, and another. This is now the fifth one."

For two days and far into each night, Dad and his companion, Pastor Albert, taught the villagers. Exhausted, they finally asked—as was customary—for permission to return home.

"Have you finished telling us all the stories?" the old man inquired.

"No, but I will return and tell you more," Dad promised.

A look of pain passed over the old man's face. "I will be dead by that time," he said. "You must stay and tell us all of the stories." Calling to several of the younger men, he had them carry him to the village cemetery, motioning to Dad to follow. The old man pointed out the graves, one by one. He explained that the people in those graves had waited, each of them, for the good news. Alas! No one had come to tell them.

"Where have you been for these many years?" the old man inquired over and over. "Where have you been?"

The good news of Jesus Christ is a treasure beyond description. On every continent there are people waiting yet to receive it. Many are going out into eternity with no knowledge of Jesus Christ, the *only* Savior, the Treasure that we bear.

But notice also that Paul says it is not enough just to take the Treasure to people. We must take care that the message of Jesus Christ is undistorted. We must send forth the truth of the gospel accurately, plainly, understandably.

For us Westerners going into another culture, our most likely distortion of the gospel will be inadvertent. Unconsciously, we burden the pure gospel with our Western trappings. Cross-cultural communication does not take place in a vacuum. We are speaking to people whose experiences and concepts are very different from our own. Every missionary entering a new culture has to discover a relevant approach for presenting the gospel. It may be some system of belief that serves as a bridge into the gospel. It may be some facet of the people's folklore that foreshadows the missionary's redemptive message. It may be some hope passed down for generations that a foreigner will bring them a long-awaited message.

In his book, *Peace Child,* Don Richardson tells how he sought for some good way to communicate the gospel to the Sawi tribespeople of Irian Jaya, Indonesia. Those aborigines needed to understand the gospel in terms of their own culture.

Don and his family were living in an area of three villages, each so antagonistic toward the others that they fought at the least provocation. In the space of two months, Don and his wife, Carol, counted 14 battles fought within sight of their home. Finally Richardson told the Sawi, whose entire culture seemed locked into ceaseless combat, that he was moving his family to another place.

"Don't leave us!" pleaded one of the Sawi warriors.

"But I don't want you to kill each other! answered the missionary.

"We're not going to kill each other," responded the speaker. "Tomorrow we are going to 'sprinkle cool water' on each other." To "sprinkle cool water" was the Sawi idiom for making peace. So the next day Don and Carol watched from their house to see what would happen.

To their horror, they saw Kaiyo, a warrior with whom they were acquainted, give his only son, Biakadon, as a peace offering to his enemies. But the Richardsons discovered, to their relief, that Biakadon would not be sacrificed. In fact, it was imperative that he stay alive. Giving this boy as a "peace child" settled past grievances and canceled future instances of treachery—but only as long as the "peace child" remained alive.

Richardson had found a key to communicating the gospel in a way the Sawi tribespeople could understand! He started with Isaiah 9:6 "To us a child is born. . . . / And he will be called . . . / Prince of Peace." He quoted John 3:16 and Romans 5:10 "If, when we were God's enemies, we were reconciled to him through the death of his Son, how much more, having been reconciled, shall we be saved through his life!." He closed with Hebrews 7:25: "Therefore [Jesus] is able to save completely those who come to God through him, because he always lives to intercede for them." Richardson presented Jesus Christ as the ultimate Peace Child.

When I went to Vietnam, I learned how to communicate the gospel to Vietnamese by listening to Pastor Phan dinh Lieu. Pastor Lieu was a former actor and the church's most effective evangelist. I spent hours listening to Pastor Lieu preach. I learned Vietnamese customs, word pictures, proverbs, folklore and even humorous stories that could be bridges to gospel truth. To pick up imagery and metaphors, I studied Vietnamese history and folklore. Instead of using Western illustrations from my background, I began using Vietnamese illustrations. My audiences would sit in rapt attention. I had removed the "foreignness" from the gospel.

Vietnamese people place tremendous importance on filial relationships, honoring their ancestors for generations back. To dishonor parents or grandparents is a cardinal crime. I discovered that Jesus' story of the prodigal son communicated powerfully to the Vietnamese mind.

Paul says we have this treasure to share with a lost world. He adds that Satan is working hard to blind people to the light of the gospel of the glory of Christ. By "setting forth the truth plainly" we can, by God's help, thwart Satan's devious intentions.

Are you manifesting clearly the truth of God's Word? Or are you distorting the message God has given us to proclaim? Are you reflecting the glory of Christ in the gospel? Or are you veiling the truth? It matters not how clever or articulate or logical or candid or funny *you* are. The value is in the Message, not the container. Are you clearly manifesting God's treasure to people?

As I already mentioned, we dare not rely on our own human resources for this assignment.

2. Missionaries Must Work in the Power of God

We have this treasure in jars of clay to show that this all-surpassing power is from God and not from us. (4:7)

A.W. Tozer, whose reputation for turning a phrase is matched by his godly wisdom, has this comment:

The popular notion that the first obligation of the Christian church is to spread the gospel to the uttermost parts of the earth is false! Her first obligation is to be spiritually worthy to spread the gospel.

Our Lord said, "Go ye," but He also said "Tarry ye," and the tarrying had to come before the going. Had the disciples gone forth as missionaries before the day of Pentecost, it would have been an overwhelming spiritual disaster, for they could have done no more than make converts after their own likeness. This would have altered for the worse the whole history of the Western world. It would have had consequences throughout the ages to come.

Theoretically the seed, being the Word of God, should produce the same kind of fruit regardless of the spiritual condition of those who scatter it. But it does not work that way! The identical message preached to the heathen by men of differing degrees of godliness will produce different kinds of converts. It will result in a quality of Christianity varying according to the purity and power of those who preach it.[2]

It could hardly have been said better! Without God's power nothing of eternal value transpires. With God's "all-surpassing power"—with the divine enabling of God's Spirit in our lives—we can minister effectively and fruitfully to the glory of God.

An example of the Spirit's power and control came out of my stint in Hong Kong. During my first year of preaching at Kowloon Tong Alliance Church I diligently prepared messages, worked hard every day and preached my heart out. But scarcely anything happened. Not one sinner came to Christ. There was very little numerical growth in the congregation and very little spiritual growth among the members. I was about to quit and go elsewhere.

One day in desperation I went to my knees instead. I cried out to God for help. God showed me a whole new strategy for evangelism called Evangelism Explosion. EE brought new life, new dynamic to my ministry. As God took over with His plan, His power and His control, amazing things began to happen. In four months 40 people received Christ. Within eight months 80 had received Christ. It was not my doing. I had totally failed! It was God taking over and exercising His power.

Pastors of other evangelical churches in Hong Kong took notice. They came to me with their questions. "What are you doing right?" "What is your secret?"

I decided to hold a special clinic open just to pastors, missionaries and church leaders. It turned out to be the first EE Leadership Training Clinic for the entire continent of Asia. EE's executive vice president, Archie Parrish, flew from Fort Lauderdale, Florida, to lead the clinic. My responsibility was to equip sufficient trainers in our local church so each church leader and missionary could have field experience in the community. Sixty-four people from all over Hong Kong had signed up for the clinic. Training enough lay people to go around was a formidable task. But God helped us. When it came time for the clinic, we had the needed lay trainers.

The next major test was to find sufficient prospects for the teams to call on. EE emphasizes referrals: people who have visited the church or people referred by members of the church. But to keep our weekly EE training on schedule for the clinic, we were already calling on all the church visitors. Unless God did something miraculous, we would not have a single prospect for the clinic's on-the-job training!

The Sunday before the clinic, we had an unusually large number of visitors at our church. And people of our congregation submitted lists of friends, relatives, work associates and neighbors whom they wanted us to visit. Some of them even helped us by calling the people on their lists and making appointments for the visit! When the clinic ended, we were not short one prospect nor did we have one prospect left over. God had supplied the exact number we needed!

As a result of that clinic, many people came to Christ. In fact, our next door neighbor received Christ and is today an elder in the church!

Clay pots have no power for ministry. But God has "all-surpassing power." Are you relying on your own ability? or have you turned your life and ministry over to God, the All-Sufficient One?

3. Missionaries Must Yield to Painful Processing by God

To experience God's adequacy, each of us needs to go through God's processing. Probably nothing in this book is as important as what I'm going to share with you next. I hope you will read and reread it. If there is a truth or a principle that I consider the secret to fruitful missionary life and ministry, it is what follows in the rest of this chapter. Paul says next:

We are hard pressed on every side, but not crushed; perplexed, but not in despair; persecuted, but not abandoned; struck down, but not destroyed. We always carry around in our body the death of Jesus, so that the life of Jesus may also be revealed in our body. For we who are alive are always being given over to death for Jesus' sake, so that his life may be revealed in our mortal body. So then, death is at work in us, but life is at work in you. (4:8-12)

Paul certainly was honest! He didn't live or minister in some ivory tower away from the ugly realities of life. Look again at how he described the context of his life and ministry: "hard pressed," "perplexed," "persecuted," "struck down," "the death of Jesus . . . in our body" "given over to death for Jesus' sake."

As believers, we have access to the greatest power in the universe: God's all-surpassing power! But what is it that releases such amazingly wonderful power? Death. We are to identify with our Lord Jesus in His death.

This means that by faith we recognize that when Jesus died upon the cross, we died with Him. Our old self-life, our fleshly desires, our earthly ambitions, our worldly intentions died there on that cross. By thus dying we remove the obstacles that hinder the free flow of God's life and power into our lives.

Notice that this doesn't happen just once. It is continual. "We always carry around in our body the death of Jesus, so that the life of Jesus may also be revealed in our body." That is New Testament life and ministry! That is Christ living and ministering in and through us! That is the key to victory, to fruitfulness, to biblical success!

It is a matter of choice, a matter of the will. We decide to live that kind of a life and to engage in that type of a ministry. But it is also a matter of circumstance. By that I mean that our everyday situations behind which our sovereign God is at work force us to experience death in various ways. We can only experience Christ's resurrection power and fruitfulness after identifying with Him in His death. Jesus said, "Unless a kernel of wheat falls to the ground and dies, it remains only a single seed. But if it dies, it produces many seeds" (John 12:24).

In Chapter 5 I alluded to this experience of death in relation to the self-life, my personal goals, earthly comforts and natural desires. I described some of the pain of saying good-bye to family, friends and comfortable American living. But death didn't stop there. It took on the form of serving, sacrifice and suffering.

As the Vietnam War escalated and physical danger increased, I had to come to the place where I also died to my physical welfare. I remember so well a message by Oswald Sanders, noted missionary statesman and author.

Dr. Sanders spoke to us missionaries and pastors at a spiritual retreat held in the highland city of Dalat. As he spoke about being willing to live or die for Christ, I realized that I might be called on to actually die physically for Christ. On my knees before God I wrestled in prayer for a long time. I didn't want Donna, my lovely wife, to be widowed. I had children for whom I wanted to live and provide. I wanted badly to continue the ministry God had given me.

But as I prayed and wept and slowly died, I finally came to the critical moment. "Lord," I said, "if I go on living in this body and don't surrender my physical life to You for Your control and use, whether by life or by death—If I go on like this without dying in this area of my life and ministry, I will be of no use to You." There at Dalat, Vietnam, the floor wet with my tears under the chair where I had been kneeling, I surrendered. Not until later did I realize what God was preparing me for.

As the days and weeks stretched into months and years, God took Donna and me through many dangers and close encounters with death. Had I not worked through it on my knees up at Dalat, I doubt that I could have, like Paul, "carr[ied] around in [my] body the death of Jesus, . . . always being given over to death for Jesus' sake."

Donna and three-year-old Janice were alone one night at our house in Danang. I was in

Saigon attending an executive committee meet-ing; our three older children were out of the country in boarding school. From time to time the Vietcong had fired rockets and mortars on Danang, but they chose that particular night to unleash one of their worst-ever aerial attacks. More than 100 enemy rockets and mortars landed on Danang, a good number of them in a ring around the house where Donna and little Janice were huddled. On all sides Donna could see homes in flames. Within a stone's throw she could hear the screams of terror-stricken mothers and children. God brought peace to her heart in the knowledge that back home Christian brothers and sisters were praying. God spared our house. And God spared Donna and little Janice.

Other missionaries died martyr's deaths in Vietnam. My sister, Ruth Thompson, and her husband, Ed, were two of six who died by en-emy fire in Banmethuot. Earlier a missionary medical doctor, Ardell Vietti, together with two other missionary workers, Archie Mitchell and Dan Gerber, were taken captive, never to be heard from again. All told, 14 missionaries in Vietnam died from enemy fire or in enemy captivity, nine of them missionaries with The Christian and Missionary Alliance.

On February 1, 1989, the anniversary of my sister's death 21 years earlier, Donna and I flew to Banmethuot with another missionary couple for a graveside memorial service. Ruth and Ed

Thompson had died in a bunker—in the ground—therefore I thought it appropriate to have John 12:24 engraved on the marble marker: "Except a corn of wheat fall into the ground and die, it abideth alone: but if it die, it bringeth forth much fruit" (KJV).

Since then, that verse has become very precious to me. In agriculture the buried seed brings forth manifold new life. So it is in spiritual life and ministry.

4. Missionaries Must Evidence Progress and Fruitfulness in God

Paul boldly, clearly, gloriously states this principle of death and fruitfulness:

> We who are alive are always being given over to death for Jesus' sake, so that his life may be revealed in our mortal body. So then, death is at work in us, but life is at work in you.
>
> It is written: "I believed; therefore I have spoken." With that same spirit of faith we also believe and therefore speak, because we know that the one who raised the Lord Jesus from the dead will also raise us with Jesus and present us with you in his presence. All this is for your benefit, so that the grace that is reaching more and more people may cause thanksgiving to overflow to the glory of God. (4:11-15)

As I stated, Donna and I have served 25 years overseas as missionaries and more recently in ministry at home. We know of no principle more evident than this one of death, life, progress and fruitfulness. I have made several references to our three-year pastorate in Hong Kong. Allow me one more.

The church had one building, one board and one budget but two separate congregations. One was Cantonese-speaking and the other was English-speaking. When I was called to pastor the English-speaking congregation, I discovered it comprised some 60 very elite, highly educated, affluent people. All of them had studied abroad. Most of them spoke better English than I. As I recall, 13 of them had doctorates—earned doctorates—in various disciplines.

I had a bachelor of science degree in Theology from what was then very small Nyack Missionary College. You can imagine how threatened I felt! To compound the problem, as I said earlier, our first year of ministry was fruitless. Self-doubt flooded my heart and mind. I wanted to throw in the towel.

What did I do? I died! I went before God and told Him that He knew better than I that I was inadequate for the task He had given me. I was going to die to the whole thing: the impossible situation, the fruitlessness, the desire to measure up and please the members. I told Him I was taking my hands off. Only He could resurrect my ministry and give me fruit. Then I asked Him for a vision of what He wanted done.

It would be inaccurate for me to say that God visited me as He visited Peter on the Joppa rooftop. But by His Spirit He gave me a deep, visionlike impression that He was going to do something new, exciting and different! As I prayed and mused about the whole matter, God seemed to be promising three things. One, He would cause the church to grow. So much so, in fact, that all the pews would be filled— even the pews in the balcony! Two, by His grace the church would become a center for evangelism and the training of church leaders for evangelism. Three, He would give our church a missionary vision; our church would send witnesses across the border into the People's Republic of China.

As I waited before God for His direction, He sent Buddy Gaines into my life. Buddy was an OMS missionary whose family attended our church. While in the States three years earlier, Buddy had been trained in Evangelism Explosion. Since then he had been praying earnestly that God would raise up a pastor in Hong Kong to implement the ministry of EE among the Chinese. Buddy was expecting God to raise up a Chinese; instead, God put His hand on me— an American who didn't know more than three words of Cantonese!

The exciting details of my EE experience in Hong Kong are in my earlier *Evangelism by the*

Book. Let me just say here that God did exceedingly more than I could have dreamed or envisioned. Donna and I remained at Kowloon Tong Church two more years. Paul speaks of God's grace "reaching more and more people" (4:15). So it was in Hong Kong. The pews filled up, both on the ground floor and in the balcony! Pastors from all over the city and from three neighboring countries came to our church to be trained in evangelism. In fact, Kowloon Tong Church became the first EE clinic base for all of Asia. From there the EE equipping ministry spread to almost every major country in Asia. God led our son, Jeff, and his lovely wife, Beth, to take EE training. They have served in the Mainland, teaching English and making disciples.

All three facets of the "vision" God gave me for our ministry in Hong Kong became reality beyond our wildest dreams!

5. Missionaries' Motives Must Be Praise and Glory to God

All this is for your benefit, so that the grace that is reaching more and more people may cause thanksgiving to overflow to the glory of God. (4:15)

Paul testified that the daily death he experienced made it possible for Christ's resurrection power to be unleashed. And that resurrection power produced fruitfulness in his life and ministry. It brought abundant, eternal life to increasing numbers of people.

Because it was undeniably not Paul's doing, God alone deserved to be thanked. Because God's grace was at work, He deserved the praise and the glory!

During our very first term of service in Vietnam, I received an invitation to preach on a Sunday morning in the village of La Hai, some distance from where we were then living. A few days after I had agreed to go there and speak, the Vietcong infiltrated our province in force. Several people were ambushed and killed on the very mountain pass over which I needed to travel to get to La Hai.

I wrestled with the decision to go or stay home. There was no way to contact the village to cancel or postpone the engagement. I knew many Christians would walk great distances to be at the church. If I wasn't there as promised, they would question my credibility.

Normally when I traveled on a weekend assignment, I was besieged by Vietnamese friends wanting to go along for the trip or to see friends. This time, not a person volunteered to accompany me. It was ominous.

In the end, I decided this was an opportunity to lay my physical life on the line, even as I had done earlier by faith. Donna agreed. So we prayed together, committing our lives to God for His purposes and will.

As I drove off alone up Highway One in my Jeep wagon, I had plenty of time to think and to commune with the Lord. I recommitted myself to Him, for life or for death—but I also told God I hoped it would be for life! After all, I was a husband and a father and a missionary whose task did not yet seem to be completed.

As I neared the mountain where the enemy ambushes had taken place, my heart began to pound. In fact, it seemed as though my heart had rapidly moved into the area of my throat! A mile or so from the beginning of the ascent to the pass, the sun peeped over the horizon. Off to the left I could see the road winding up the mountainside—the road I soon would be turning onto.

Just as I came to the turnoff, something amazing happened! A light rain began to fall. And those raindrops blended with the rays of the morning sun to form one of the most beautiful rainbows I have ever seen. And guess where it was? God dropped it like an archway right over the mountain pass I was about to traverse! To me, at that anxiety-filled moment, it had to be as beautiful and meaningful as the first rainbow that God sent to Noah.

With the glorious, reassuring sight of that rainbow, my heart dropped back to where it belonged. A deep peace flooded my being. "God is there at the pass!" I exclaimed to myself. "And He'll be with me the rest of the journey."

He was.

I totally forgot about communist guerrillas and any other impending dangers that might have awaited me. I had a good ministry at La Hai. The next day I returned to Donna, still in one piece and very much alive, praising the Lord for His great goodness to me.

In these "clay pots," if they belong to God, is precious treasure. The ordinary vessels merely serve to accentuate the power of God indwelling them. Through God's sometimes painful processing He enables us to progress and be ever more fruitful. The result? Praise and glory to God!

That is how every true missionary and every Spirit-anointed worker in God's kingdom wants it to be.

Study Guide Questions

1. What kind of people does God often choose and use as missionaries? Why?

2. In what three ways are missionaries like clay pots?

3. What treasure do "clay pot" missionaries hold and carry?

4. What may missionaries do to discover relevant approaches for presenting the gospel to people of another culture?

5. What act on the part of the missionary (or

lay Christian) releases God's amazing power?

6. Should this be a once-for-all or a repeated exercise? Is it a matter of choice or circumstances? Explain.

7. To what does such a process lead? What does it produce?

8. Why does such a New Testament lifestyle and ministry bring praise and glory to God? How?

Endnotes

1. Quoted by Charles Swindoll, *Growing Strong in the Seasons of Life* (Portland, OR: Multnomah Press), 87.

2. A.W. Tozer, *Renewed Day by Day* (Camp Hill, PA: Christian Publications, 1980), December 14 reading.

Chapter Thirteen

A Balanced Home Base

Acts 1:8

IN EARLY 1956 DONNA AND I WERE appointed by The Christian and Missionary Alliance as missionaries to Vietnam. A year later, January 11, 1957, we set sail from San Francisco on the *S.S. Steel Navigator.* As a third generation missionary and a second generation missionary to Vietnam, I fully intended to live, die and be buried in what had been the land of my birth. But a sovereign God had other intentions. On April 30, 1975, Vietnam's door to Western missionaries closed—decisively, tightly.

Donna and I were reassigned, first to Guam for a year and then to Hong Kong. We had been in Hong Kong not quite three years when Omaha Pastor Albert Runge arrived. He had been invited to minister at our annual conference of Hong Kong missionaries. Pastor Runge had used Evangelism Explosion with great success at his previous church in Burlington, Vermont. He was looking for someone to help him launch a similar outreach in Omaha. He knew that Donna and I were soon to leave Hong Kong for furlough. He could sense our enthusiasm for EE Al Runge invited me to join his staff in Omaha.

A number of considerations influenced our decision to accept the call. We were attracted by Pastor Runge's personal commitment to evangelism. The Omaha church's missionary zeal was well-known. Like Paul's compassion for perishing fellow Jews (Romans 9:1-3; 10:1), we felt compassion for perishing fellow Americans. Omaha's location in the geographic center of the continental United States meant we could reach out in every direction! We felt we had fulfilled the vision God gave us for Hong Kong. Our children were at a critical age; we considered it unwise to leave them alone in the United States.

But another consideration was determinative. On our furloughs Donna and I had seen an imbalance in many of our home-base churches. Some churches went all-out to reach the ends of the earth, but did little to evangelize lost people nearby. Others zealously evangelized at home but had only token interest in reaching lost people around the world. That concerned me! I sensed a divine leading to do something about that imbalance.

So it was that after 25 years in overseas service, Donna and I found ourselves at the "home base."

I can testify that both Donna and I felt as clearly led to Omaha as we had felt led to Vietnam 25 years earlier. And God gave us a vision for Omaha as unmistakable and biblical as the visions He had given us for Vietnam, Guam and Hong Kong.

Not everyone, of course, understood that the same God who led us to *go* was now leading us to *stay*. A well-meaning woman in Pennsylvania remarked to Donna, "Now that you're not going to be missionaries anymore, I won't be praying for you. So please take my name off your mailing list." Like that!

This is the final chapter of *Missions by the Book*. It is fitting that we conclude it by considering what it means to be part of a missionary-sending church. If God has called you to be one of the sent ones, I pray that you will follow through. You are needed! Indeed, you may already be an overseas missionary. On the other hand, you may be reading this book with no expectation of going overseas—not even to visit! You may therefore be tempted to think of yourself as a "second-class Christian." You may consider yourself not quite as worthy as those missionaries who serve abroad. Nothing could be farther from the truth! David, who led his troops to victory over the Amalekites, set a policy for Israel: "The share of the man who stayed with the supplies is to be the same as that of him who went down to the battle. All will share alike" (1 Samuel 30:24). Those who maintain the home base are just as necessary as those who are on the front lines. Without frontline troops *and* a base of support and supply, there can be no victory.

To understand the proper balance for home-base churches, we must turn again to the Book. A person doesn't have to read far in the New Testament to discover that Christ gave marching orders to His church. We generally refer to those orders as the Great Commission. On seemingly five distinct occasions Jesus stated His orders in differing words. Each evangelist reports one of the times. The Acts reports yet another.

God, who everywhere graces His great creation with glorious symmetry, does the same in His Great Commission. As a God who loves balance, He longs to see His people, His church and His work kept in balance.

In Mark's account of Christ's Great Commission, the emphasis is on evangelism: "Go into all the world and preach the good news to all creation" (Mark 16:15). That is balanced in Matthew by an emphasis on edification—the building up of the believers: "Go and make disciples of all nations, baptizing them in the name of the Father and of the Son and of the Holy Spirit, and teaching them to obey everything I have commanded you" (Matthew 28:19-20).

Luke adds other important facets of the balanced message we are to proclaim: "This is what is written: The Christ will suffer and rise from the dead on the third day, and repentance and forgiveness of sins will be preached in his name to all nations, beginning at Jerusalem. You are witnesses of these things" (Luke 24:46-48). Luke adds to the message Christ's death and resurrection and people's need to repent and be forgiven. He also adds the need for the messengers to wait until they "have been clothed with power from on high" (24:49).

John reports still a different, but well-balanced model of the missionary task that Christ passed on to His followers: His *peace* ("Peace be with you!"); His *pattern* ("As the Father has sent me, I am sending you"); His *power* ("He breathed on them and said, 'Receive the Holy Spirit' "); and His *pardon* ("If you forgive anyone his sins, they are forgiven") (John 20:21-23).

Then, just prior to His ascension, Christ commanded a very crucial geographical balance (Acts 1:8). It is a balance that any healthy home-base church will want to follow. Christ first reminds His followers of their need for *power.* He promises: "You will receive power when the Holy Spirit comes on you." He tells them their *message* is to be Himself: "You will be my witnesses." Then He outlines their ever-expanding *plan for witness:* "In Jerusalem, and in all Judea and Samaria, and to the ends of the earth." It is this geographical expression of the Great Commission that I want to focus on as we search for a balanced home base.

On July 1, 1980, Donna and I arrived in Omaha prepared to begin our Stateside ministry. Pastor Runge introduced me as the new "Minister of Evangelism." Later I asked him if we might broaden the title to "Pastor for Outreach." I felt that *evangelism* was too narrow a word for the more balanced approach I envisioned for the church. I also was concerned lest the word *evangelism* "frighten the fish." If I called in the home of unbelievers and announced myself as an "evangelist," I might unnecessarily put the family on the defensive. Then, too, in the spirit of Ephesians 4:11-12, I preferred to think of lay people as the "ministers" and myself as the pastor-teacher-equipper.

Aware of my wide experience, Pastor Runge graciously asked me to draw up my own job description. I recommended to him that in broad strokes our evangelism follow Jesus' Jerusalem, Judea, Samaria, ends-of-the-earth pattern. To lead our "Jerusalem" outreach, I would be responsible for visitor relations, personal evangelism training, discipleship of new believers and social service ministries. To reach our "Judea," I would lead EE clinics for Stateside pastors and church leaders and help in the church-planting efforts of our district. At the time, I didn't fully see the large ethnic population of Omaha as a possible "Samaria," but that's the direction God led us. Finally, to reach "the ends of the earth," I would give leadership to our church's world missions thrust.

Before I expand on the outworking of those broad objectives, let me mention three very basic principles. These principles have guided me as I have worked to build what I like to call our church's "Great Commission" outreach.

The first is *prayer*. At 6 a.m. every Saturday morning, a group of 4-10 men gather with me not for Bible study or socializing, but prayer. We spend the first few minutes sharing answers to prayer and then go right to our knees. The prayer requests for the various aspects of our church's outreach are printed on two sides of a sheet of paper. We move around the circle, each one praying for three requests. It is a disciplined experience. We are in battle for people's eternal lives, for the advance of Christ's kingdom and for God's glory.

God has given us some wonderful answers. Whatever our church has accomplished in evangelism, discipleship, church planting, social service or missions has been in answer to prayer.

The second principle is *planning*. We now call it "Masterplanning." Before moving to Omaha, our present senior pastor, Bob Thune, was trained by Bobb Biehl, president of Masterplanning Associates International. Bob Thune trained me, and I, in turn, have trained elders and deacons who have become responsible for the various aspects of our outreach ministry. Ministry belongs to the laypeople. That is my conviction. So I spend the major part of my time enlisting, equipping, delegating, coordinating, inspiring and refining according to a master plan we have together agreed on.

The third principle is finding *people with a passion*. Before launching any ministry, I want a lay person in charge who is passionate about that particular ministry. For nearly 10 years I wanted to reach the over 700 international students on Omaha's college and university campuses. Then a young businessman, Don Dugger, whom I had trained in EE, walked into my office and introduced a student from Africa whom he was hosting in his home. Instinctively I knew that Don was the leader I was looking for. For six months Don and I met together once a week. I trained him and together we developed a master plan for student ministry. The work expanded so much under the leadership of Don and his wife, Becky, that the church has appointed a full-time staff person, Julie Arant, to handle the load.

With those three principles in mind, let me tell you what we have done at Christ Community Church to develop a biblically balanced home base.

1. "Jerusalem"

For Christ Community Church, "Jerusalem" is greater Omaha and its environs, a population of some 500,000. We view these people, many of whom are lost, as our responsibility. We have a passion to reach them with the gospel.

Concerning the people of greater Omaha, Christ Community Church has this mission statement: "To make disciples of Jesus Christ by winning people to faith in Christ, building them through the Word of Christ and equipping them to fulfill the Great Commission of Christ." Does that sound a bit like Jesus' last command? We like to think of ourselves as a "Great Commission" church.

One condition I stipulated for my coming to Omaha was that I train all the leaders—pastors, elders, deacons—in EE. They, then, would be equipped to lead the rest of the congregation in evangelism. When it came right down to the wire, a few leaders didn't want to be trained and eventually left the board. They were replaced by members with a heart for the Great Commission.

The leaders whom Donna and I trained joined us in training other members of the congregation. Today over a thousand members of the church have been EE equipped to reach our Jerusalem for Christ. Not everyone is able to take 16 weeks of intensive evangelism training. So we developed a shorter course to help members reach particularly their *f*riends, *r*elatives, *a*ssociates and *n*eighbors (FRANs). Four times a year we offer in every New Community Group (what we formerly called Sunday school classes) a Bible lesson on how to pray for and reach out to FRANs. Then, usually two to four weeks after that special evangelism lesson, we offer our congregation an outreach event geared especially to the unchurched. We call the times of these special events FRANtastic Days. It may be a choir concert at Christmas or Easter coupled with a short evangelistic message or an outside speaker with a subject calculated to appeal to non-Christians. All this equipping and outreach has revolutionized our church!

In New Testament times, the gospel seems to have been communicated primarily through the natural networks of friends, relatives, associates and neighbors. We sensitize our members to this potentially responsive network they have and to their responsibility to share the gospel with these "FRANs." We have discovered that people concerned for their FRANs have usually an equal concern for lost people in other lands. That, in a nutshell, is what we mean by a balanced home base.

I should add that this emphasis on evangelizing our Jerusalem and reaching our FRANs produces missionaries! A number of our members who were trained in EE are today on most of the continents serving Christ as missionaries.

Whenever our outreach is productive, we disciple the new believers. We have two tracks under the direction of our discipleship elder: a one-on-one Bible course at the convenience of the new convert, and a seven-week "New Beginnings" class. All seven lessons are offered every Sunday. A new convert can begin the series the very next Sunday, and participants who miss a Sunday can pick up the lesson the following week.

2. "Judea"

"Judea" for Christ Community Church in Omaha is both the denominational "district" the church is in and the whole of North America. One of the long-range goals of Christ Community Church is to impact other churches in North America and abroad. One way we have done this is to host EE Leadership Training Clinics. In Omaha and on site worldwide, I have now had the privilege of training almost a thousand pastors, missionaries and church leaders for effective evangelism.

A pastor in Hawaii brought his wife to a June clinic at Christ Community Church. Half a year later I received a Christmas card from them. The wife had enclosed a note. She said she had personally experienced the joy of leading to Christ a couple who had just arrived in Hawaii from—Omaha! And in six months since she and her husband attended our clinic, their congregation had doubled!

Another way our church has sought to impact our Judea is through church planting. Planting churches costs money! So at our annual missions conference we give our people opportunity to supply some of that money for our district's church planting efforts. Just as they pledge money for overseas missions, they pledge money for church planting in their district. Each year the people have given more and more generously to reach out at home. The figure is now over $60,000 annually!

On its own, Christ Community Church has done some church planting. Council Bluffs, Iowa, just across the river from Omaha, was our first project. With a nucleus of 10 interested church families, it seemed to be off to a good start. But then, one by one, the families started moving away—one to Texas, another to Florida, still others to California. Only three of the 10 families were left. Then Al and Brenda, our leading couple, announced they were planning to move back to Des Moines, Iowa.

The night Al and Branda told us that, Donna and I drove home from Council Bluffs completely discouraged.

"Sweetheart," I said to Donna, "tonight I die to this new church planting effort. I'm finished. I bury it, once and for all. If God wants to resurrect it and make it go, that's up to Him."

The next week we went back to wrap things up. But to our surprise, Al and Brenda had changed their minds. "We've prayed all week about our move," they said, "and have decided to stay here and help you get this Council Bluffs church going!"

I had buried the project, but God had begun the resurrection process!

New families began to join the group every week until we were forced to move to a rented hall. The district found a pastor willing to lead the fledgling church. Ian Hoover, from Texas, proved definitely to be God's man. A layman from Christ Community Church gave over $90,000 to help us purchase 11 acres of prime land on Council Bluff's main street. The church raised money to construct a lovely building with additional space for Christian education. Attendance is now over 200 on Sunday mornings—all to the glory of God who exercises His resurrection power even in the realm of church planting!

To date, Christ Community Church has had a part in planting 15 churches in the greater Omaha area, including 3 ethnic churches. None has adversely impacted on the growth of the mother church.

Related to church planting has been my efforts to reproduce myself in younger workers. Over the years in Omaha I have been able to give on-the-job training to selected ones, preparing them to be outreach pastors, church planters or missionaries. As I train them, I ask each of them, in return for the training they receive, to help me with our local church planting ministry. Three of these are now outreach pastors in Florida, New York and Washington State. Three others are church planters in Iowa and Nebraska.

3. "Samaria"

For us at Christ Community Church, "Samaria" refers to the ethnic Americans living in greater Omaha. The Samaritans of New Testament times differed ethnically from the pure Jews of Jerusalem, Judea and Galilee. They were half Jew and half Gentile. That Jesus had compassion for them is evident from His witness to the Samaritan woman at Jacob's well (John 4).

America is rapidly becoming a multi-cultured nation. In almost every community are people of differing ethnic backgrounds. As Great Commission churches, we should be working to reach them for Christ. Christ Community Church takes very seriously its responsibility to the ethnic population of Omaha. It has geared its outreach strategy to include these ethnic minorities.

With my Vietnam background, you can be sure one of my first concerns was to have a witness to and plant a church among the more than 1,000 Vietnamese in our city. A Vietnamese seminary student, Nguyen thanh Phien, served as a summer intern with me and translated the EE material into Vietnamese. Together we conducted a clinic for the many Vietnamese pastors and lay leaders in North America. As a result of the clinic, a number of local Vietnamese put their faith in Christ Jesus. We gathered these on Sunday evenings for a Vietnamese worship service. Soon we were able to call a Vietnamese pastor to shepherd the group. Today the church numbers over 70 and continues to impact the local Vietnamese community.

Omaha has a black population of 80,000. Christ Community Church had sent 10 missionaries to black Africa but none to black Omaha. That concerned me. Our Saturday morning prayer group began praying for a church among the unchurched Afro-Americans in Omaha.

I began to study existing black ministries in Chicago and Atlanta. I visited with pastors in and outside my denomination. Planting churches in the black community is difficult, extremely difficult. The usual approach of a home as a meeting place and a bi-vocational pastor does not work. Starting a black church requires money—plenty of money. Establishing some sort of a related social service ministry is a must. To make matters harder, nonblacks need not apply as pastors. A black church requires a black pastor who understands the nuances of black culture.

But what would be the shape of the initial social service organization that in turn would lead to a church? A group of interested members at Christ Community Church began meeting regularly to pray. As they prayed, they also planned. And they established an official steering committee. They came up with the acronym COMPASS Ministries: Christian Outreach to Multicultural People Assisting with Social Service. Finally, in 1990, the ministry was incorporated with a multicultural board at the helm.

Three months later Greg Williams and his wife, Ernestine, came to lead the ministry. Greg was no novice. He had served more than 13 years in the U.S. Air Force, then graduated from Crown College, St. Bonifacius, Minnesota. As soon as Greg arrived in Omaha, he started ministering in the local correctional center, counseling, teaching classes, networking with other black churches and looking for a building in the target area.

We held fund-raising banquets and were able to purchase a modern building that provides street-level offices and ministry space for COMPASS and a lower-level worship center/fellowship hall capable of seating 125. A new congregation of some 25 people is now in its formative stages.

As COMPASS grows and expands, Greg has a vision to impact Afro-Americans in other cities of our church district: Kansas City, Denver, St. Louis, Des Moines, Wichita. We are praying that COMPASS might be a model for other districts in our denomination.

Our prayer group has also prayed long and fervently for a witness among the Hispanic population of Omaha. Even as I write, it looks as though that prayer is about to be answered.

International students are another sizable ethnic group in Omaha. We prayed for several years concerning this group. And the Lord of the harvest raised up a layworker to direct this ministry. We call our ministry FOCUS—Friendship to Overseas College and University Students. While these students study here in Omaha, we want to host them in our homes and our church. We want to reach out to them with a loving and relevant witness. Various couples in our church have started inviting students to their homes for holidays or weekends. We have a Bible study in simple English during the Sunday school hour. Each quarter the church provides a potluck dinner for these students after the Sunday morning worship. There are other bridge-building social activities as well. Member interest in the international students has been growing. We are believing God for a fruitful ministry.

Some of the students are from countries such as Nepal, closed to Western missionaries and the gospel. Some of the students are destined for positions of political power in their countries. All can share the gospel among their peers. International students are a very important segment of America's ethnic mix.

Recently something happened that points up another benefit of our ministry to international students. One of our church's missionaries, because of a visa denial, couldn't return to his place of service. Don, at the time our deacon in charge of FOCUS, was hosting in his home a student from that same country. He mentioned to his guest the visa difficulty.

"My father is the official who signs all of those visas," the student replied brightly. "I will call him immediately and ask him to work out the difficulty for your missionary!"

Only God knows what influence this FOCUS ministry will have upon the work of Christ overseas in future years. Outreach to our Samaria, we feel, is of utmost importance to a balanced home base.

The last and most distant sphere of witness referred to by our Lord is . . .

4. "The Ends of the Earth"

Christ Community Church understands "the ends of the earth" to mean world missions—taking the gospel cross-culturally to other nations. Our long-range goal is to give a million dollars annually to world missions and to send from our church 100 career missionaries. In addition, every year we endeavor to send and support scores of short-term missionaries. We have sent junior high youth to Mexico. We have sent senior highers to the Dominican Republic and Puerto Rico. We have sent college youth to various countries with groups such as the Alliance Youth Corps. Our adults have gone out with Alliance Men, Walk Through the Bible and Evangelism Explosion.

We aim to involve every person in our church in world missions. All can pray, all can give at least something. And many can even go. To see that aim become a reality, we promote missions all year long in various ways.

We elect a missions elder who is responsible for the general oversight of missions in the church. He chairs an elected missions committee of some 30 people. A key member of the committee is the elder who serves as missionary treasurer. He is responsible for raising, monitoring and reporting all money given for missions. Six other members oversee, respectively, the annual World Missions Festival, missionary education, short-term missions projects, missionary hospitality, missionary recruitment and the care of our non-Alliance missionaries. Six "members at large" are elected by the elder board. They generally are men and women with a long-standing commitment to and involvement in missions. Finally, each of our 18 Sunday school classes elects a representative to serve on the missions committee. If letting Sunday school classes be represented on the missions committee seems like a strange arrangement, let me explain.

By now Christ Community Church is *large.* Some 2,500 people attend on a typical Sunday morning. Being a large church, we feel it is important to break down the "bigness" by having within our congregation a number of smaller "churches." Our 18 Sunday school classes serve that purpose. They are, however, much more than Sunday school classes. In addition to the customary Bible lesson, each class has other activities: socials, care groups, home Bible studies, prayer groups, outreach groups. In fact, as I mentioned before, we no longer call them Sunday school classes. We call them New Community Groups. The representative each of these groups elects to the missions committee serves as a representative from his or her group. He or she also is in charge of missionary education within the group he or she represents.

Our annual World Missions Festival, held after Easter each spring, deserves some additional comment. We purposely named it a *festival* because we wanted it to be much more than just a missions conference. We endeavor to make it really a festive occasion that everyone will want to a part of. The deacon in charge of the Festival works the year around to prepare for it. He enlists 12 coordinators who help him plan and organize the entire Festival. Eight months before the event, each of these enlists a group of volunteers to assist in various facets of the Festival: prayer for its success, decorations, ethnic dinners (one for each weekday evening), hospitality, booths and banners, drama, music, costumes, promotion, book table, the participation of youth and children. These coordinators are given a job description, a report form, a budget and a progress chart to help them implement their tasks. With those tools, only three planning meetings are necessary: a "kick-off" meeting early on, a meeting a few weeks before the Festival to make sure everything is on track, and an evaluation meeting two weeks after the Festival ends.

Our goal is to involve as many of our congregation as possible. In that way they will view our world missions outreach with a genuine sense of ownership. For example, a New Community Group will be involved in preparing and serving one of the weeknight ethnic dinners. Or in setting up and manning one of the 12 display booths that grace our lobby during World Missions Festival week. Or in serving as a team of greeters, dressed in foreign costume, at one of the services. By actual count we have seen more than 500 different members of the congregation in recent years actively participating in the Festival.

We purposely schedule the Festival two weeks after Easter. By then most of the furloughing missionaries have completed their obligatory "tours" of the churches. In that way, we have our pick of missionaries and can include a representative from each continent. We also invite a Bible teacher to present the Bible basis of missions. Our Festival runs from Sunday to Sunday and includes two services every weekday, one in the morning and one in the evening. Children's meetings are held during the evening services, and there is an all-day Youth Fest on Saturday.

Prayer meetings for the Festival begin many months ahead of time and continue every day during the Festival.

About a month ahead of the event, every child gets a missions bank to save coins toward a gift for the visiting missionaries. On the opening Sunday of the Festival, during the Sunday school hour, children discover a large foreign "market" set up in the gymnasium. The children exchange their coin banks for printed

"foreign money" with which they may "purchase" simple foreign food or artifacts. Market
time closes with a talk to the children by one of
the missionaries.

All year long, a large map of the world graces
the main lobby of our church. Surrounding it
are 8 x 10 color portraits of our 54 missionaries
that Christ Community Church supports financially and in prayer. On a rotating basis, we
print in the Sunday worship bulletin a photo
and prayer request from each of these missionaries. Every year we send to each missionary a
Christmas gift, a birthday greeting and—to
those who are married—an anniversary card.

You may recall that one member of the missions committee is a deacon in charge of non-
Alliance missionaries. As the number of
missionaries from our congregation increased,
we found it important to make someone responsible to address the situations unique to
these missionaries and to help them with fund-
raising within our church. Christ Community
Church does not take on the support of non-Alliance missionaries outside the church, but it
does feel a responsibility for those of the congregation who feel God's leading to serve in
some type of ministry or some country in
which The Christian and Missionary Alliance is
not active. To be a Christ Community Church
missionary, a person must meet five conditions:
(1) be a member of the church, (2) be certified
in EE, (3) be recommended by his or her New

Community Group, (4) be approved by the missions committee and elder board and (5) be appointed by a responsible evangelical missions board.

Non-Alliance missionaries are invited to present their financial needs from the platform, in the New Community Groups and by letter to their supporters in the church. At present we have a study committee seeking to discover more effective ways to help them generate support.

If the Lord does not return first, Christ Community Church has some turn-of-the-century goals. It would like to double its present 54 missionaries (serving in 21 countries). And it would like to see total annual giving to missions (currently $600,000) top the million dollar mark.

Despite all the church is doing to be a balanced home base, we realize we have not fully achieved that goal. But we earnestly desire to be just that—a biblically balanced home base. We work hard to refine what we are doing toward that objective.

You may be thinking, *That's great for a church of 2,500. Christ Community Church can be a biblically balanced missions home base. But the church I'm in is small. There's no way we can follow Omaha's example.* Remember the Chinese proverb: "The longest journey begins with a single step." Study afresh the Great Commission. Then look at your local situation to see what you can do to impact your Jerusalem, Judea, Samaria and the ends of the earth. Size is not the important thing. The quality of the commitment is what counts. Your church can become, to the glory of God, an effective and balanced home base for world evangelization.

Study Guide Questions

1. Are those who stay at home and become involved in missions at the home base "second-class" Christians? Explain your answer.

2. List five places in the New Testament where Christ's Great Commission is stated.

3. What are the geographic implications of Acts 1:8? How may they be applied to a local church today?

4. Why are *prayer, planning* and *passion* essential to a church wanting to be a balanced home base?

5. What might be your church's "Jerusalem"? your "Judea"?

6. What might be your "Samaria"? How might you reach it for Christ?

7. What steps might your church take to enhance its missionary interest and support? What can *you* do to further this goal?

8. How might you personally become a "world Christian" in the New Testament sense of that term?

A Note to the Readers

Subsequent to the completion of this manuscript, author Tom Stebbins has accepted an invitation to become Executive Vice President of Evangelism Explosion III International. This international ministry has a goal of reaching every nation of earth with the gospel.

For 15 years (1980-1995) Tom was Associate Pastor for Outreach at Christ Community Church in Omaha. Before joining Evangelism Explosion, Tom made sure he and his wife, Donna, would continue their ties with Christ Community Church.

"We requested," Tom says, "that we be released, endorsed and commissioned to [this new] ministry." Christ Community Church calls Tom and Donna their "missionaries at large with an assignment to the world."

Tom and Donna are now based in Fort Lauderdale, Florida, not in the Midwest. But they will continue to regard Christ Community Church as their "home church" and Omaha as their "home town."

"In fact," Tom adds, "when the appropriate

time comes, Donna and I are thinking of retiring in Nebraska among God's people whom we have grown to love and appreciate so much!"

Appendix

The following correspondence between Tom Stebbins and his wife was written the day before and two days after South Vietnam fell to the Communist forces. It highlights what the Stebbinses experienced during this difficult period.

6:50 a.m., April 29, 1975

Honey,

I'm fine after a rough night of bombing, rockets and machine-gun fire. I climbed the Embassy wall and spent the night with Dr. Dustin in his clinic here.

I'm going to try to get a large number of pastors and Christians out today.

Miss Nhung, Colonel Church's sister, is taking this letter out for me.

I love you worlds, and will see you soon in God's providence. Give my love to the kids, our family and friends.

God is good, perfect, His ways are marvelous

and I love Him with all my breath and strength.

What a welcome Mr. Mieng (church president) and the Christians gave me at the International church at 6 p.m. yesterday. Everything has worked beautifully. I sure do love our dear Vietnamese—all of them. I wish I could save everyone not just from the impending danger but for His purposes eternally.

Be good and if I don't make it out keep your chin up serving Him.

Your loving hubby,

Tom

May 2, 1975

Sweetheart,

I am so happy to be able to write to you—I have died a thousand deaths since I last saw you. No doubt you have passed through the valley of death many times also. Sweetheart, ever since Monday when the Chaplain called from Clark Airforce Base to say you were airborne—I said to him, "Thank you for calling me as I want to pray continuously." The afternoon you arrived in Saigon there were explosions and fighting. Mon. night Betty, Irv and I prayed, Tues. night Floyd and I prayed for you. Floyd stayed over an extra day as he had to meet Drew, Franklyn, John Sawin at airport and drive them to Clank. The 29th the airport was captured and they couldn't fly into Saigon. Drew called me several times each day, he was wonderful. Drew told me helicopters were landing on the International Protestant Church parking lot, I had visions of mobs of people fighting to board the planes and you being left behind. Or you were out in search of someone and got left behind, or were killed by a sniper—four days seemed like an eternity having you in Vietnam under communist takeover.

How I prayed and wept for you. Praise the Lord, He heard my cries and answered my prayers! Floyd left Wed a.m. Drew called me 6:30 Wed a.m. He said, "All Americans are out of Saigon, there are no U.S. left" a knife went through my heart, in a broken voice said "there is no more Vietnam." Oh, how it hurt to realize after all these years the enemy was victor. Drew continued, "We suppose Tom was flown out by helicopter and is out on a ship somewhere. Ships will reach Guam about Sunday." I went into the bathroom to cry—if I had not had guests waiting for me at the breakfast table I would have wept uncomforted.

That a.m. 30th I read in the paper that there were some Americans who were left behind—how could I be sure that you weren't in that number? Tues. night I couldn't sleep, I prayed and tossed all night, read the Bible but could *only* think of you. Drew called later in the day. I asked him, "Who are the Americans that got left behind?" he told me so I felt better. Wed. night Mr. Kerr called and he talked very hesitantly like he was holding back something from me, he said they (NY) were very concerned and were praying much, I was to call NY if I got any word from you. I couldn't sleep that night, I laid awake trying to imagine my life without you. I feel after 20 years we have only begun, I cherish every moment with you, I love you so deeply. Dr. Han Brown called to ask about you and to assure me of FEBC's prayers.

The Schlanders came Wed. at about 7:30 p.m., it was a tonic to see them and talk to them. Wed. night I was on my knees weeping and praying, I pled with the Lord to give me release, after finishing praying for you and interceding for the Vietnamese on the ships, those left behind in Saigon and everywhere—the phone rang—it was Grady, he said, "Donna, we received a radio message from Tom he is on the SS Vancouver, he left Saigon 1 a.m. the 30th." I responded, "Praise the Lord!" Grady talked so kindly and Dr. King talked to me, they thanked me for being so brave and remaining of the job. I guess they were surprised to learn that I was alone at the guest home. Mr. Kerr talked to me—they were all so wonderful! I will never permit anyone to speak against our leaders, I will stand to the defense of these men, Godly men and yet so humble and full of compassion. I will always be 100% behind the C&MA.

While these three men were speaking with me I had enough composure at 11 p.m. to talk business. I told them Schlanders were leaving for Guam on the 3rd and I would proceed to Guam when the Gibbs returned from conference. I asked about the money for Vietnamese refugees, about our captive missionaries. I thanked them for their prayers and concern and that I greatly appreciated all that had been done and was being done on behalf of our Vietnam field.

What a relief to know you were safe but I have continued to pray for you and think of you *constantly*. When I sit down to a table, take a hot shower, sleep in a clean bed, I pray for you. I fear you have been very seasick and extremely exhausted—I have so many questions. Read in the paper this a.m. there are 46 ships going to Guam with more than 40,000 refugees. What an undertaking for Guam! Dr. King told me the Reimers, Flemings, Schlanders, Stebbins maybe some others, would be in Guam.

Sweetheart, I wish I were there to welcome you. I won't ever let you go again! We belong together and it is too painful being apart. I can hardly wait to be with you! I got to thinking we might be put up in dormitories—then how will we get together when we are so busy with the refugees? Anyway, I am so thankful you are alive and free, that I am not a widow, that I can wait for privacy. LOVE YOU.

After listening to the tape will you please send it to Jennifer—the three J's talk about Jenny, one section John talks so softly, but he is speaking so keep it going. After hearing you were on the SS Vancouver I read the 4 J's, so far as I knew they didn't know about your going to Vietnam.

Everything is going fine <u>now</u>. I did not speak for Mike Harrison cause I was upset and I was waiting for phone calls. One family will come in tonight. The Gibbs return the 6th. I will probably come to Guam the 8th unless there is a change.

Much, much love,

Your wife

Books by Tom Stebbins

Evangelism by the Book
Friendship Evangelism by the Book
Oikos Outreach 4 Times a Year